BOLLYWOOD POSTERS

JERRY PINTO & SHEENA SIPPY

With 225 color illustrations

Thames & Hudson

First published in the United Kingdom in 2008 by
Thames & Hudson Ltd,
181A High Holborn,
London WC1V 7QX

www.thamesandhudson.com

First published in 2008 in paperback in the United States of America by
Thames & Hudson Inc.,
500 Fifth Avenue,
New York, New York 10110

thamesandhudsonusa.com

Original edition © 2008 India Book House

British Library Cataloguing-in-Publication Data
A catalogue record for this book is available from the British Library

Library of Congress Catalog Card Number:
2008905904

ISBN: 978-0-500-28776-7

Printed and bound in India

The Hindi film industry is held to be a cinema without genres.
However, we believe that this is an outsider's viewpoint,
the stand taken by someone importing an occidental
framework for the viewing of an indigenous cinema.

This book follows the notion that Bollywood
did have genres. Based on the general emphasis
of the plotlines involved, we have tried to
categorize the films and their posters.
Of course, some films elude easy
categorization.

It is best to think of the Hindi film
as an Elizabethan play. Just as
audiences in the 17th century expected
a little comedy, some raunch, a song
or two and a good story, Hindi film
audiences expect a film to have it all.
But it is still possible to divide
Shakespeare's plays into comedies,
tragedies and histories, and this is what we
have done too. We believe that the makers of
these films were also working in genres. If they
weren't, all Hindi film posters would look the same.

As you will see, they don't. Vive la différence!

JERRY PINTO
Mumbai

Some art forms, like paintings, are created in solitude.
Others, such as films, are the result of the effort of several
more people. This book on Bollywood poster art is a tribute
to the collaborative vision of the producers, directors,
designers, artists and photographers who created these
teasers that announced their technicolour dreams.

This book would not have been possible without the enormous
help, keen memory and honest goodwill of Mr NC Hira. You have our
deepest and sincerest gratitude always!

SHEENA SIPPY
Mumbai

INTRODUCTION

In the small space afforded to me by the window near my computer, a thousand messages wage war on each other. My mind revives them momentarily but each can only take so much of my time before my eye is dragged on to the next. This is because I live in Mumbai, the economic engine of a country of more than a billion people and the ultimate testing ground of every product, idea or message in the country.

Mumbai, the city of a million glossy Bollywood dreams, is also one of the most visually cluttered landscapes of the world. On every inch of space a Darwinian struggle for survival takes place and the combatants include political slogans ("Cast your vote for elephant"), public service messages ("Don't waste water, you'll need it later"), government diktats ("Pay income tax. Walk tall"), health regulations ("Get your child immunized"), advertising challenges ("Are you in the loop?"), a million entertainment options from music videos to new television serials and, of course, invitations to the main event: Bollywood. The posters or hoardings for Hindi films have a certain primacy. They start with an advantage over all other contenders.

India is a nation obsessed with cinema. When Dhundiraj Govind "Dadasaheb" Phalke (1870-1944) showed his first film, *Raja Harishchandra*, in 1913, India began a passionate affair with celluloid. Approximately 800 films are made every year, a large percentage of them coming out of the studios, big and small, of Mumbai. Although most of these fail, each year brings a fresh crop with no diminution in numbers. In other words, there is no economic sense in this business. It runs on glamour, on its own solipsistic appeal and on its self-generated aura. It defies economic logic and market forces even as it offers employment to about six million people and has an annual turnover of a billion dollars.

And because India is home to several languages, because it is home to nearly half the extant scripts in the world, because it speaks and loves and rants in several tongues, it is home to several cinemas. Of these, Bollywood is the star of the show, the cinema that has achieved some international attention and collected, almost by accretion, a gathering of loyal fans across the world. There are many debates around that simple term, the one the world has come to take as shorthand for a certain kind of cinema coming out of Mumbai: the commercial Hindi film.

The name Bollywood is itself contentious, of course. Some argue that "Bollywood" is a derogatory term, used to indicate that the cinematic produce of Mumbai is a derivative of that produced in Hollywood. Others accept the term but apply it to a certain kind of film alone, that which is made with only commercial intent, which takes no risks in terms of its storytelling, which uses big stars and cushions them in high production values, which drives the plot through song and melodrama, which seeks to preserve the moral and economic status quo in terms of its plots and in the resolution of the predicaments that it posits as plot devices. We use the term in this book because it is current and because it is communicative, with an affectionate acceptance of its pejorative roots and the confidence that it will transcend such condescension.

But even if we accept that there are two kinds of film made in Mumbai, the Bollywood and the art-house variety, the title of this book would stand the test. The more serious cinema (called parallel cinema or middle-of-the-road cinema) that was pioneered in the 1970s by Shyam Benegal rarely had recourse to hoardings. Their posters were generally also to be found only outside cinemas where they infrequently played. This, some might argue, was because art-house film directors did not see Hindi cinema-goers as their audience. A more elite class of viewer was sought, one that would be familiar with the nouvelle vague in France and Satyajit Ray's work in Bengal. This class of audience, they probably believed, was more likely to be influenced by critical reviews and word-of-mouth reports, than posters on the street.

An argument more in keeping with the ground realities of cinema might be that since most of these films were made with government subsidies from bodies like the National Film Development Corporation, they would have no advertising budgets or be able to afford commercial space. Nor were the producers under great pressure to recover their investments, since they were, in novelist Upamanyu Chatterjee's felicitous phrase, still suckling at the mammaries of the welfare state. Even those hoardings that were not directly related to cinema came from the denizens of the mainstream commercial industry. Each year, for instance, the vamp Bindu hired a hoarding in central Mumbai to wish her fans a very happy Diwali.

Whatever the reason, few art-house films had hoardings on the street. One of the exceptions was *Chakra* (1981, Rabindra Dharamraj), a film set in the slums of Mumbai. The protagonist of the film was Smita Patil and an image of her bathing in the open at a street tap with only a petticoat covering her body seemed central to the campaign. Perhaps this had to do with the fact that movie mogul Manmohan Shetty was the producer of this film and not the National Film Development Corporation.

But it is not just the name Bollywood that is contentious. The language is itself contentious. There are those who claim that the films are made in Urdu, that the finest thoughts and most elegant sentiments are always couched in the hybrid tongue that arose in the 16th century in Emperor Akbar's camp and which slowly rose from the argot of the barracks to the language of the salon. As Mukul Kesavan argues in his elegant essay, "Urdu, Awadh and the Tawaif" in *The Ugliness of the Indian Male*:

The prehistory of Hindi cinema is located in theatre and the language of this theatre – the Parsi theatre of the 1870s, for example – was Urdu. Any repertory company that aspired to a national, metropolitan audience, as opposed to a provincial one, had to operate in a language that had the largest possible urban middle-class reach. This language was Urdu. The same logic applied to cinema. Why wasn't this language Hindi? Because the administrative and literary traditions of Islamicate empire survived into the colonial period and received the patronage of the colonial state. Under the aegis of the British, Urdu succeeded Farsi as the language of administration in north India, just as Urdu had gradually supplanted Farsi as the language of the cultivated Islamicate elite. Official patronage and the weight of history queered the pitch for the debutant player, literary Hindi in search of its Sanskrit roots. Urdu, the language of public affairs, of the state, had more opportunities and more arenas in which to extend its range. In pidginised form, it became the vernacular of the Indian army; it was the language of law and justice. When the Anglican missionaries translated the Bible for a North Indian readership, they rendered it into Urdu.

Although Kesavan continues over several persuasive pages to make the case for Urdu, anyone familiar with the bloody history of the subcontinent will know that there are too many colonialisms underlying this history to make it easy to accept. And finally, just to make things a little more difficult, Urdu borrowed its grammar and its syntax from Hindi, linked to it in a symbiotic relationship.

While scholars and practitioners debate the nomenclature, *those* films in *that* language simply continue to be made and consumed and win new audiences across the world. Each year, 3.6 billion people watch Bollywood films across the globe but each film must first prove itself in its home city, with local audiences, before it seeks its fortune in far-off lands and on other alien screens.

Whether filmmakers and film distributors admit it or not, Mumbai is the psycological test. Perhaps it has something to do with the film industry being located here, against all odds. (Hindi, Hindustani or Urdu are not native tongues. Northerners laugh at the way the Mumbaikar speaks "their" language.)

Perhaps it has something to do with the western-facing seaport being the economic engine of the country, therefore the place where fashions explode and implode first, the city that is always the first to take on a fad and the first to discard it. Perhaps it has something to do with driving down the roads and seeing your own poster plastered on the walls. In his autobiography, Dev Anand records his excitement at seeing a representation of himself on a railway platform:

One day, as we were travelling together by train in Bombay, Guru Dutt suddenly gasped, looking at a poster on the station platform.
'That's you!' *Hum Ek Hain* was about to be released. The posters were up. By the time I looked back, the local train had moved on, and I could only see the poster as it passed out of sight. I could not register anything of its contents.
'It'll probably be boring for you, but I'd like to get back and see myself hanging at a railway platform, like I had seen Ashok Kumar's banner once!' I told Guru Dutt.
He agreed to indulge me. We came back in the same train without getting off, and postponed the proposed destination we were off to, to a later time.
Standing at the railway station, watching my face on a movie poster for the first time, with a few people staring at it with pleasant curiosity was a thrilling experience. I looked at Guru Dutt – He smiled and simply said, 'Good.'

From ROMANCING WITH LIFE by Dev Anand

And although Hindi cinema has been fairly niggardly about representing itself, there is a moment in *Main Madhuri Dixit Banna Chahti Hoon* (2003, Chandan Arora) where the young Chutki (Antara Mali) stands in front of her first film hoarding and looks at herself up there outside a theatre. This is a moment to be cherished but, as she discovers, it is also a moment that could end in the cruel laughter of a jaded Mumbai audience.

This audience, with its savage post-release comments, is what the poster must seek. It does begin with some advantages. The nation's best-known faces peer out of these posters. They are among the best paid of Indians, thus adding the ineffable power of money to the already potent combination of physical beauty and success. They are, as film scholar Raymond Durgnat says, "a reflection in which the public studies and adjusts its own image of itself".

Every Bollywood film gets a once-over from potential ticket-buyers, even if it is only to check which stars are involved or to reassure themselves that none are. Other consumer products may camouflage their advertising in order to resemble Bollywood posters and hoardings, hoping for the rub-off effect. And, of course, there are celebrity endorsements, equally divided between cricketers and Bollywood stars, although the latter are seen as more dependable since their fortunes do not fluctuate with each match. When there are several films being released almost every week, the Bollywood poster must compete against itself. It must send out a powerful message. It must shout. Much of the sheer melodrama you see in the pages that follow is part of the economic imperative of attracting the attention of a heterogeneous mass of people and redefining them as a public audience.

Over the years, what public has that been? In poster after poster across these pages you will notice that the language is English. Yet, for many decades filmmakers maintained that they made films for the "masses". When a director was asked about the melodrama with which he had concluded a film or the improbability of some plot development or even a failure in continuity, he would simply take refuge behind the catch-all excuse: "My film was made for the masses." The masses was a codeword for the illiterate Indian, the man in the stalls, the man who squatted on the unfamiliar seats in a theatre, often the man who would donate his blood to afford seeing a film.

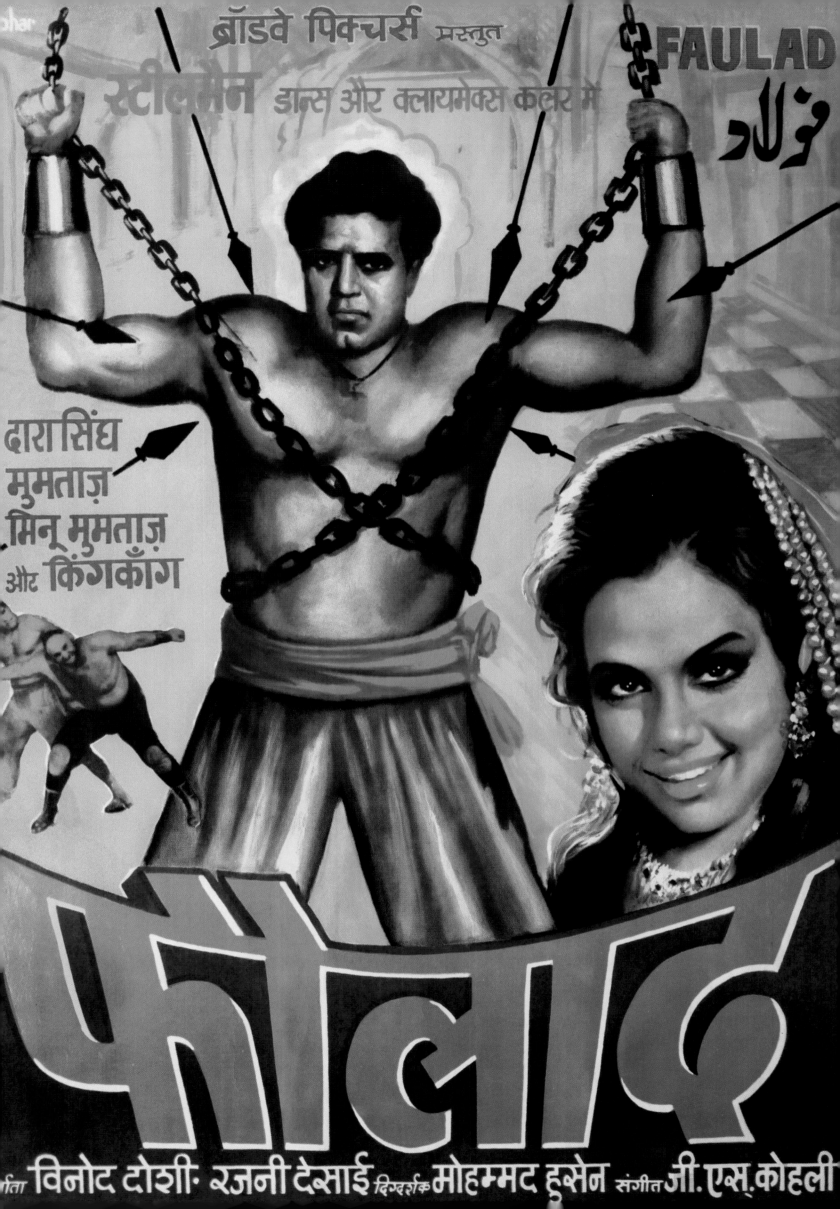

TIPS INDUSTRIES LTD PRESENTS
TIPS FILMS
DIRECTED BY
PRODUCED BY KUMAR S.
A UTV MO
indiatimes
58888
sms RACE to 58888
for mobile downloads
www.race.tips.in

One of the all-time greats of commercial cinema, Manmohan Desai (1936-1994), said:

I don't make my films for critics. I make them for those people who are willing to stand hours in the sun and rain to buy a ticket. If they are unhappy with my film, I am unhappy too, and I would like to apologise to them.
From ENCHANTMENT OF THE MIND: MANMOHAN DESAI'S FILMS by Connie Haham

Desai and all the other filmmakers like him, those who made the big films that they hoped would have pan-Indian appeal, knew that the masses could make or break a film. They were the ones who brought in the money, who carried a film into its 25th or 50th week. They would come for the repeat value, often to watch some song again or to enjoy a sequence more fully, laughing in anticipation of a punch line in a comic interlude, their bodies flinching in the fight scenes.

But in many a Bollywood heart, I suspect, there was a longing for critical acclaim. Filmmakers were aspirational in the sense that they wanted the middle class watching their films. English was one way of reaching the unreachable. The other might be that the illiterate masses would have their own way of "reading" a poster. A symbolic language was developed: a gun might mean a thriller, a rose might mean a romance and caricatures would signal a comedy. From the faces that dominated the posters, they would know who the stars were and they could decide whether they wanted to see the film or not. The poster in English was probably meant to target the undecided, to convince those who could not be swayed – or would pretend not to be swayed – by the lurid appeal of the stars. Each poster was an invitation to a specific feast. Thus it would need to throw the highlights of that feast into prominence. Most often, this is not a complex decision. The stars come first, simply because they are stars. There may be other imperatives such as the use of a star to stabilize audience response, as Hollywood film writer Alexander Walker suggests.

To these may be added the specificity of the film's story or dramaturgy. If the heroine of the film has worn something revealing – a low-cut blouse, a short skirt that suggests a hint of underclothing, a bikini – this gets fore-grounded. But even the heroine's pulchritude will take second position to the hero. It is generally his face that is given the maximum space on a poster but this has often been expanded now to include his body.

Like all other forms of advertising, the poster too responds to its environment. Advertising as a medium has its own aesthetic but also responds to art movements and the *zeitgeist*. When *Bobby* was launched in 1973, one of the most stunning posters devised for it had the lead pair as a couple of stylized figures on a psychedelic background. Nothing in the film had anything to do with what psychedelia actually meant: no one tripped, no one used drugs to expand their consciousness, there were no allusions to flower power or any of the holdovers of the 1960s that filtered through into the 1970s. But the typography and the stylization had another function which was symbolic. It was an indication that this would not be the common-or-garden Hindi film but one that was "modern".

Modernity had been defined in those days as westernization. One of the pioneering films about the encounter between East and West, between what was seen as traditional Orient as opposed to morally corrupt Occident, was *Hare Rama Hare Krishna* (1971, Dev Anand) in which the hero (Dev Anand) goes to Nepal to track down his sister (Zeenat Aman) who has joined a bunch of pot-smoking hippies. It was probably this connection the psychedelia hoped to emphasize, the link between the young and rumours of the uninhibited sexual practices of hippies.

Perhaps it might be better to look at *Bobby*'s film history. The legendary director Raj Kapoor (1924-1988) had had his heart broken when his magnum opus *Mera Naam Joker* (1970) flopped at the box office.

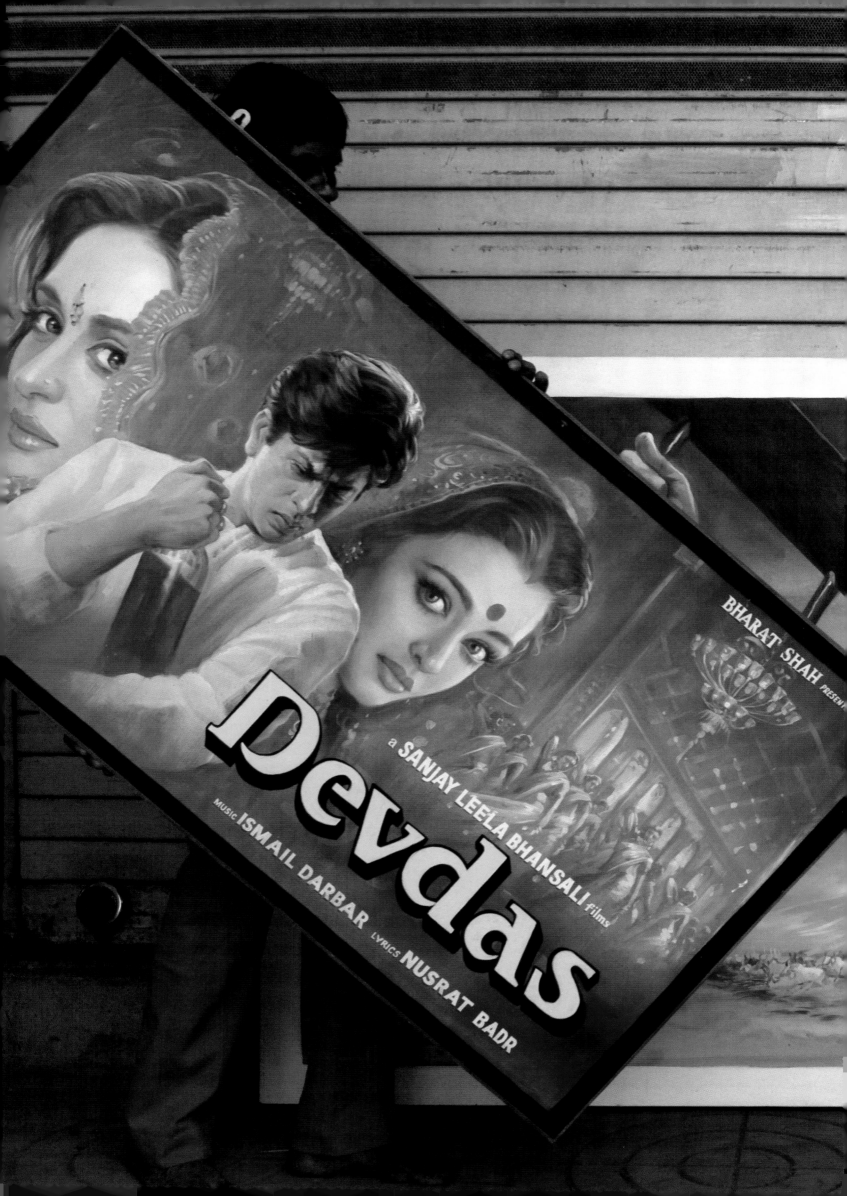

He had thrown himself into it, he was the joker whose heart was sad behind his smile, and though this self-indulgent monster of a film has now acquired a cult following, at the time it had brought his studio RK to its knees. *Bobby* was made as a film that abandoned all the artistic principles – an interest in social justice, the romanticization of poverty, the glorification of the Indian farmer and worker – the studio had stood for. It was the sell-out film and after that, RK continued to rely on the male gaze, on exploitative representation to sell its films.

Thus *Bobby*'s poster constituted an offer: the viewer would get a film in which there would be young women in short skirts and tight clothes, or the even more erotically charged dress of the tribal woman. All this is to remind the reader, if such reminder is needed, that a poster is not just a free-floating signifier of an aesthetic or an industry. It is an artefact with a visceral connection to a certain specific film and its fate will be linked to the fate of the film, for better or worse.

When *Zanjeer* (1971, Prakash Mehra) was released, its first posters starred Jaya Bhaduri, then a successful film star with several releases to her credit. This should have been counter-intuitive since the film dealt mainly with the angst of the hero Vijay (Amitabh Bachchan). Vijay's parents are killed when he is a child. He is brought up by a police officer and becomes one himself. He is a maverick cop, fuelled by his rage against crime. It is his quest for vengeance that dominates the film. But when *Zanjeer* was released, Bachchan was not a star. He had had seven flop films and no doubt the producer felt that *Zanjeer* would have a better chance of attracting crowds if they played up the female lead.

As almost everyone knows, this was the film that inaugurated the reign of Amitabh Bachchan as a superstar, heralded the arrival of the Angry Young Man and reinvented the notion of the cinematic fight. Later posters and hoardings in the second-run theatres would feature Bachchan's face almost to the exclusion of the film's other actors.

Often a film's fate will determine what happens to its posters and this is not just a matter of their value as collectibles. In order to boost an uncertain film's success, the producer might order a barrage of Hit and Superhit posters with which to create an aura of success.

But it isn't always puffery. Mega successes may generate other posters, subsidiary ones. In the old days when a film ran for several weeks, producers would order a new poster for the silver jubilee (25 weeks) or the golden jubilee (50 weeks) or even the platinum jubilee (75 weeks). In recent years, these have only been ordered for *Dilwale Dulhania Le Jayenge* (1995, Aditya Chopra), which has spent 12 years as a matinée in Maratha Mandir, a cinema hall in central Mumbai. Many say that this is as much a function of its qualities as a film as it is of being a tax-free film, in an area where an air-conditioned hall and a clean toilet might draw in a huge number of people from the working class for a cool three hours at minimum cost.

Today many of the old verities about the Hindi cinema audience have evaporated. Posters may be in English simply because a Hindi film may actually be targeting what is now called "a multiplex audience". As Ram Gopal Varma, maker of films like *Satya*, *Company* and *Rangeela*, has told *Time Asia*, "With my films, I'm targeting the urban multiplexes, the sophisticated media-savvy young crowd. Frankly, I couldn't give a f*** for the villages."

This is an English-speaking, aspirational class of young people who enjoy Hindi cinema but also enjoy world cinema, available through hundreds of rental agencies and thousands of pirated films. Cynics claim that the ubiquity of world cinema in Mumbai can be attributed to the plagiarism that plagues Bollywood. For whatever reason, the best is available in Mumbai now at the click of a mouse. This new audience

BHUMIKA

Patil

UN FILM DE SHYAM BENEGAL

is visually much better educated. It cannot be fobbed off with knock-off posters of western or other releases. It expects design as part of the offering.

Whatever way you look at it, the Bollywood poster was designed for a very public space. It was meant to be seen from a distance, at a certain height on a lamp-post, behind glass outside a theatre.

The poster was designed only to part the punters and their paise. This was its central function. If we have forgotten how powerful the poster once was, it is because the ways in which films are talked about have multiplied exponentially. The first intimation is often on the Internet; new television channels will play their part, airing pre-release specials; radio talk shows help publicize the films; indeed, every film lists its media partners at the beginning of the film. The poster is now just one of the ways in which a film may be publicized. This has also contributed to the nostalgia that adheres to posters.

Removed from their environment, the hardworking posters of Bollywood may seem like exotic artefacts. They are. This is what gives the poster-as-painting, the poster-as-interior-design-element, the poster-as-collectible, so much of its charge. It is at home in our homes because these images have found a way deep into our psyches; it is completely alien to our living rooms because it was not so very long ago that Bollywood was a secret passion with the upwardly aspirational middle class. This was a top-down situation. By 1954, you could no longer hear Hindi film music on the national radio

service, All India Radio. This drove all those who had drawn emotional sustenance from the film song to the competition, Radio Ceylon. Many observers have seen this as a Brahminical response to what was considered the bread and circuses of popular cinema.

It is easy to blame the upper-caste contempt for popular forms but it must be remembered that in general the middle classes have also always had an ambivalent relationship with popular forms. Many of the pioneers of cinema were treated with contempt. That they began to earn good money early on in the game did not make up for their lack of social acceptance. The very fact that movie actors were earning so much – the silent movie star Sulochana was supposed to be making more than the mayor of Bombay in the 1930s – was proof to the middle classes that something was wrong.

Also, it is only recently that middle-class homes have begun to be designed to showcase the tastes of the owners or inhabitants. Until a few years ago, the walls of most homes were covered with religious imagery or photographs of the family at various important rites of passage. A few might have added a lithograph or some sample of the homemaking skills of a daughter, such as a piece of embroidery or a harmless watercolour. A film poster would be unthinkable.

You can tell that this is so because very little critical attention has been paid to the Bollywood poster. Its aesthetic has gone unremarked, its inclusion into the pantheon of the collectible has gone

BACK TO BASICS: The hero of a Hindi film often turns his back on the accepted code of his times and carves his own path. These poster designers have obviously both conceived the same idea for two different film stars in two different films

रेखा

SHARMILA TAGORE · SHATRUGHAN SINHA in

KEWAL ART
PRODUCTIONS'

DO
SHATRU

EASTMANCOLOR

PRODUCED & DIRECTED BY   MUSIC
KEWAL MISRA · KALYANJI-ANANDJI

uninterrogated. Its function in public life has gone unnoticed. Its lifecycle from information ("A film is to be released and it will star the following people") to mnemonic ("A film has been released and is showing close to you") to symbol ("A film has been released. It has been successful enough for us to release it again"), has gone unexamined. That it can have within it, at the stage when it is information, certain symbolic resonances (the presence of a flag, a religious icon), that it can have at its mnemomic moment certain new information (the addition of a song, often a way of bringing audiences back to the theatre), that it may arrive at another life stage when it hangs on the wall of a suburban house, seems to have been ignored.

And yet the poster has had a vital role to play, as may be seen in these completely unrelated events.

When *Rocky* (1981, Sunil Dutt) was released, the traffic police requested the producer and director, Sunil Dutt, to take down the posters that were on the Mahim Causeway, a stretch of road that links the island city of Mumbai with the northern suburbs and the hinterland. The sight of the young Tina Munim in a bathing costume – albeit a one-piece costume – was causing too many accidents. This was odd since Sharmila Tagore got into a bikini as early as *An Evening in Paris* (1967, Shakti Samanta), thus lending considerable star power – she was seen as a Satyajit Ray discovery and related to the Tagore family which named among its luminaries the painter Abanindranath and the poet Rabindranath – to the notion that the heroine could wear a bikini and still get her man.

In the late 1970s, Yash Chopra was driving through the city, he says, and he had an epiphanic moment. Everywhere, he saw posters of men doing violent things, waving guns and hitting each other. "My eyes grew tired on that drive," he says. "I thought: I want to make a love story." And he went out and made *Chandni*, the first of a series of films that would foreground romance.

When a political party wishes to demonstrate its moral standing as a guardian of the morality of India, or an upholder of Indian culture, it will target a film – and its most easily available symbol, its poster. Although every Indian film that finds commercial release has already been censored in accordance with the Indian Cinematograph Act of 1952, the blackening of a film's posters that has offended some ideological group or the other is one form of censorship that is routinely exercised by the mobocracy. This kind of attack has been levelled against Deepa Mehta's *Fire*, for instance, in 1998, for its depiction of a homosexual relationship between two Indian women.

While this book does not purport to offer a full-length study of the subject of posters, even supposing such a study could be fruitfully encompassed within the ambit of a single book, the creators hope that it will raise some questions. So what does a Bollywood poster on a wall out in the open mean? And what does it mean when it is no longer a public artefact but re-inscribed into the home space for private consumption? How does the woman with the gun turn from an invitation to a debauch to an invitation to a giggle? Why is it that we prefer the poster-as-art to the poster-as-photograph? Why is it then that our favourite Bollywood posters come from a time when design was not such a self-conscious element of the processes of marketing or creativity? What does it mean when a young person hangs the poster of a film she has not seen, in her living room? Has this process of commodification finally purified the poster, divorcing it or severing it from its context and its history? Is the love of kitsch sufficient justification for this severance?

If our heroine's eyes follow you around the room, it may be because she has some questions she wants you to answer.

At gunpoint.

DRAMA

B *oot Polish* graphically shows the problem of destitute children, their struggle for existence and their fight against organised beggary. The purpose of this film is to bring home to you that these orphans are as much your responsibility as that of the Government. Individual charity will not solve this problem because the only solution is cooperative effort on a national scale.

Raj Kapoor, quoted from a newspaper advertisement, WHY I PRODUCED BOOT POLISH

It was a time of capital letters, a palmy time, the golden age for Indian filmmaking. The 1950s were, by common consent, the decade when art matched commerce perfectly. The great film directors and producers of the time would not have understood the notion of the Bollywood movie, of the art-house movement, of middle-of-the-road cinema. They were very sure that they were making art, telling stories and entertaining people.

They were also sure it could all be achieved in the same film. You can see this in the way that Guru Dutt mounted his films, designing the light with extreme care. He also instructed his music directors that there should be no musical introduction to the songs in his films, so that song would segue seamlessly from dialogue or spill out of a character's lips on an impulse. Mehboob Khan wanted to create an India of Nehru's dreams: where dams would be the modern temples and Hindu and Muslim would live together in mutual tolerance.

But they were also patriarchs, these men who decided the shape of Hindi films as we know them even today. They were paternalistic, they were status quo-ist and they were definitely male. They did not see their audiences as co-authors; they saw them as receptacles. They underlined everything because they were sure that the illiterate masses needed to have everything explained to them. And to this end they used melodrama.

The source of most Indian melodrama is unjustified suffering. In *Waqt* (1965, Yash Chopra), which can claim to be India's first multi-star film, Lala Kedarnath (Balraj Sahni) seems to be at the pinnacle of success when it is all taken away from him by a natural disaster. The family is finally reunited but only in a courtroom where one of Kedarnath's three sons is being tried for murder. The focal points of the film are the three sons of the merchant and the poster designer has stacked them in order of seniority in the frame. None of them meets the viewer's eye; they gaze out of the frame to the left as if seeing something or someone approach.

This makes the *Waqt* poster something of a rarity. In most others, the star looks straight at the viewers, offering the intimacy of eye contact. This has always been very important in India, as Christopher Pinney points out:

Within Hindu practice, the enormous stress on visuality endows a great range of images with extraordinary power. A key concept here is of *darshan*, of 'seeing and being seen' by a deity, but which also connotes a whole range of ideas relating to 'insight', 'knowledge' and 'philosophy'.

From PHOTOS OF THE GODS: THE PRINTED IMAGE AND POLITICAL STRUGGLE IN INDIA by Christopher Pinney

In the poster for *Ankhen* (1968, Ramanand Sagar), the eyes of the hero meet ours squarely but there are two other eyes in the loops of the letters too. These suggest the duplicitous life of the spy played by Dharmendra.

The suffering on which most melodrama was predicated could be personal, as it is in *Yaadein* (1964) made by Sunil Dutt, a single-actor film in which the other roles are played by voices, shadows and, in one case, balloons. *Yaadein* begins with the protagonist returning to an empty home one evening, and ends with the coming of morning.

But the films that left a deeper impact were those in which suffering transcends the individual case. In *Jis Desh Men Ganga Behti Hai* (1960, Radhu Karmakar), Raju's loss of innocence is much more powerful because he, like the nation, had begun to lose faith in the ideal of socialism. When the naïve Raju allows himself to believe that the dacoits are socialists, he is setting himself up for a fall. The equation was simple and even more powerful because it was not clearly stated: those who had said they would create an equal society turned out to be wolves in ideological sheep's clothing. This disturbance is reflected in the poster which seems to have a peculiar Van Gogh quality in its brush strokes, as if the poster painter were trying to reproduce the delirium of elm trees on the Gangetic plain.

In general, though, it is the women who suffer. The poster for *Swami* (1977, Basu Chatterjee), therefore, is an intelligently executed deception. One might think that Saudamini (Shabana Azmi) has been relegated to the floor by her *swami*, a word that means "husband" in colloquial use but which also carries the suggestion that an Indian woman's husband is her god. In reality, she is sleeping on the floor as an act of protest against a marriage into which she has been forced. But eventually it is she who manages to realign the family and restore her husband (Girish Karnad) to the status that he deserves. The poster for *Khamoshi* suggests female suffering with the bars and fences that cut off the nurse (Waheeda Rehman) from the patient with whom she has fallen in love (Rajesh Khanna). The film itself was one of the few to articulate in words the notion that a mother figure is extremely important in the lives of men. (Indian cinema's Oedipal Complex is well-documented but it is always implicit, never stated.) And while the psychiatrist in charge of the hospital does not actually invoke Freud, he suggests that the loss of the mother figure sends men out looking for the same kind of acceptance.

A.A.N. PRODUCTIONS' NARGIS IN

RAAT AUR DIN

रात और दिन
رات اور دن

SATYEN BOSE

DIRECTED BY SATYEN BOSE

MUSIC SHANKER JAIKISHAN

All of which points to the importance invested in the figure of the mother. This is in complete consonance with the patriarchal nature of the Hindi film, where mothers, sisters, daughters and wives, if servile, are all treated as being perfect and blameless. This assumption does not apply to other women, especially those who are not constrained by family bonds. These are the vamps, the bad women, the fallen angels who lurk in the corners of the posters.

The woman at the centre of one of the most famous posters ever is Nargis playing Radha, the daughter of the soil, the woman who will pull her own plough, the embodiment of rural suffering. *Mother India* (1957, Mehboob Khan) is perceived as one of the great symbols of motherhood, not just because Radha sacrifices her personal happiness at the altar of the good of the community but because she could be identified with the nation. In creating *Mother India*, Mehboob Khan may have fulfilled a need.

Oddly enough, Indian mythology, epics and Sanskrit drama have no portraits of the Great Mother from which Indian cinema could draw inspiration. Sita in the Ramayana is the great wife; so is Draupadi in the Mahabharata. Gandhari, aged mother of a hundred Kauravas, could have been one, but never shaped up to it. She did mourn their loss on the battlefield but the dominant impression she gives is of wifely loyalty as she goes about in a blindfold. Her husband does not have the use of his eyes; so the wife deprives herself of hers. Ahalya is turned first into stone by her son's curse on her trespasses and then back into human form by Rama's touch. Damayanti goes through her suffering for Nala as does Saivya for Harishchandra. Parvati's asceticism wins her a great husband in Shiva; Savitri's single-minded devotion to her husband defeats death. The examples are too many to recount.

From THE PAINTED FACE: STUDIES IN INDIA'S POPULAR CINEMA by Chidananda Das Gupta

Mother India represents the apotheosis of suffering femininity. The polar opposite is the good-time girl. The poster for *Raat aur Din* (1967, Satyen Bose) indicates the difference clearly. The vertical split makes the distinction between Peggy (Nargis) and Varuna (Nargis) clear. While Peggy wears a dress, flaunts a cigarette and meets our gaze with a "come hither" look, Varuna is dressed as a bride and looks away. *Raat aur Din* was an Indian version of *The Three Faces of Eve* (1957, Nunnally Johnson) in which Joanne Woodward played the split personalities of Eve Black, Eve White and Jane. Nargis was thus playing the first screen heroine to be affected by multiple personality disorder. In case we had any lingering doubts about where our sympathies were to lie, Varuna's share of the poster is white while Peggy stands barefoot in the darkened half. And while the film was sympathetic to her plight, it was also quite clear that there was a moral at work here, a moral that needed to be underlined, so that even those who looked at the poster would not be able to miss it.

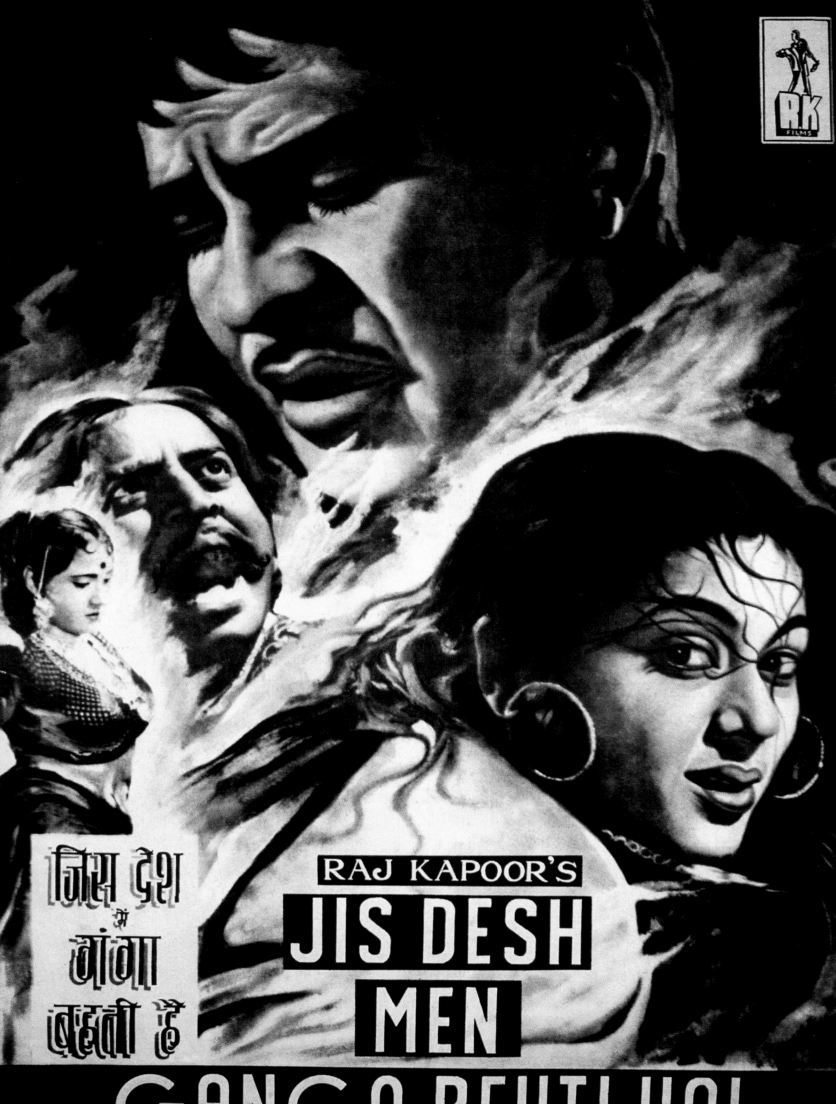

DHARMENDRA
HEMA MALINI
PRAN
AND
MEHMOOD
in

Naya Zamana

in EASTMANCOLOR

PRODUCED & DIRECTED BY
PRAMOD CHAKRAVORTY

MUSIC
S.D. BURMAN

LYRICS ANAND BAKSHI WRITTEN BY SACHIN BHOWMICK • GULSHAN NANDA • AGHA JANI KASHMIRI

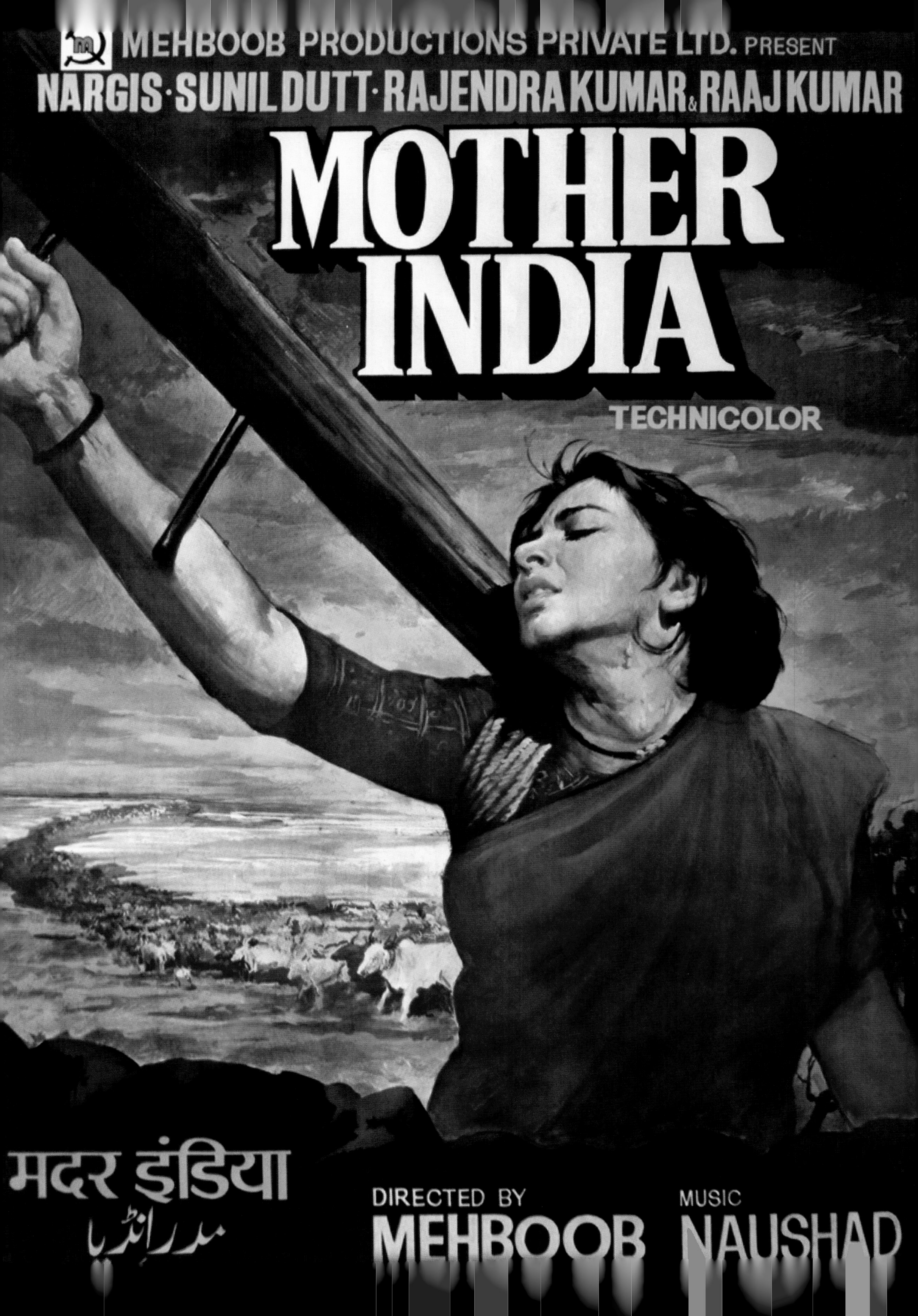
MEHBOOB PRODUCTIONS PRIVATE LTD. PRESENT
NARGIS · SUNIL DUTT · RAJENDRA KUMAR & RAAJ KUMAR
MOTHER INDIA
TECHNICOLOR
मदर इंडिया
مدر انڈیا
DIRECTED BY
MEHBOOB
MUSIC
NAUSHAD

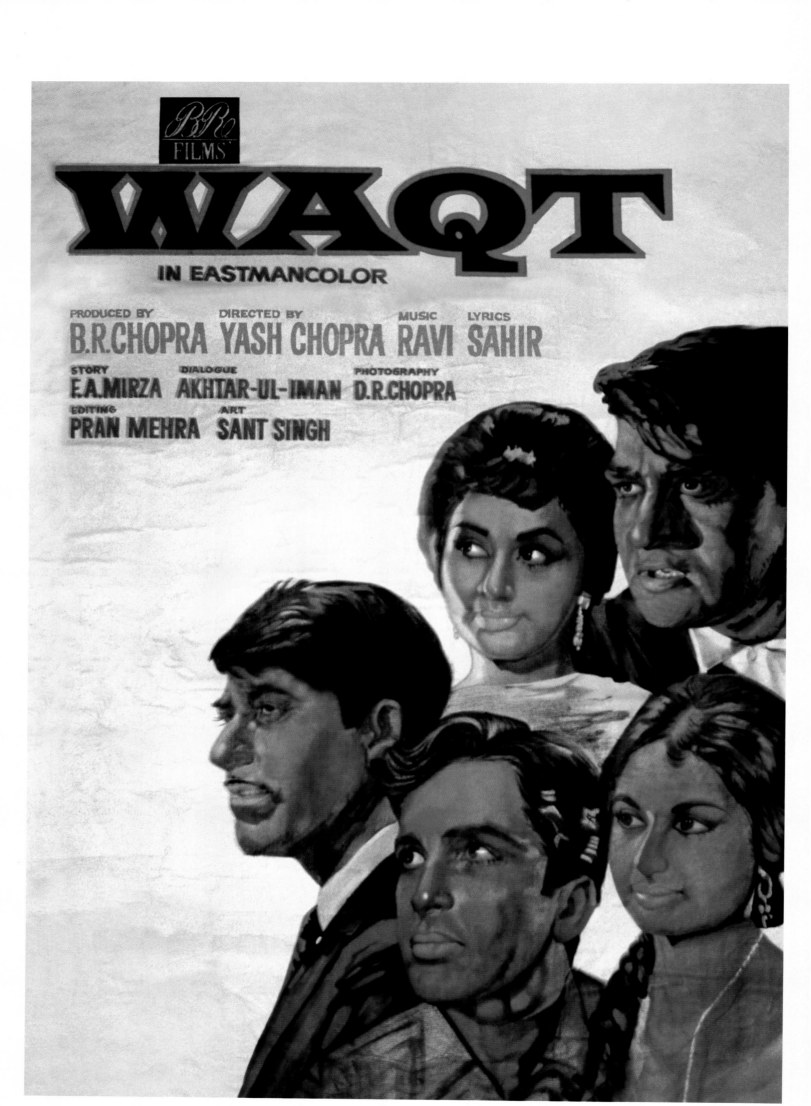

RAJ KAPOOR'S

MERA NAAM JOKER

TECHNICOLOR

PRODUCED RAJ KAPOOR
DIRECTED & EDITED BY RAJ KAPOOR
WRITTEN BY K. A. ABBAS MUSIC SHANKAR JAIKISHEN

MEENA KUMARI
DHARMENDER
RAAJ KUMAR
PADMINI
MUMTAZ
MEHMOOD

KALPNALOK'S

Kaajal

EASTMANCOLOR

काजल كاجل

PRODUCED BY DIRECTED BY LYRICS MUSIC
PANNALAL · RAM MAHESHWARY · SAHIR · RAVI

CINE PRINTERS, DELHI-35

वाडिया फिल्मस
कृत

दिलीपकुमार नर्गिस
जीवन

मेला MELA
ميلا

दिग्दर्शक एस. यू. सन्नी संगीत नौशाद

MEHBOOB PRODUCTIONS PRIVATE LIMITED PRESENT

NOORJEHAN SURENDRA & SURAIYA

ANMOL GHADI

DIRECTED BY MEHBOOB MUSIC NAUSHAD

अनमोल घड़ी
انمول گھڑی

RAJ KAPOOR'S

श्री ४२० SHREE 420

PRODUCED & DIRECTED BY RAJ KAPOOR   WRITTEN BY K.A. ABBAS   MUSIC SHANKER JAIKISHAN

JAYASARTHY COMBINE presents

SARAT CHANDRA'S

Swami

eastmancolor

A FILM BY BASU CHATTERJEE

MUSIC RAJESH ROSHAN LYRICS AMIT KHANNA CAMERA K.K.MAHAJAN PRODUCED BY JAYA CHAKRAVARTHY

MEHBOOB PRODUCTIONS PRIVATE LIMITED present

DILIP KUMAR · NARGIS · RAJ KAPOOR

ANDAZ

अंदाज़
انداز

DIRECTED BY
MEHBOOB
MUSIC
NAUSHAD

PRITISH NANDY COMMUNICATIONS
PRESENTS
KAREENA KAPOOR
RAHUL BOSE
CHAMELI
Two strangers. One stormy night.
DIRECTOR OF ART OMUNG KUMAR DIRECTOR OF PHOTOGRAPHY ASEEM BAJAJ MUSIC SANDESH SHANDILYA PRODUCED BY RANGITA PRITISH NANDY DIRECTED BY SUDHIR MISHRA
A PNC FILM
© copyrights PRITISH NANDY COMMUNICATIONS LTD. 2003

SAHIB BIWI GHULAM

THE ETERNAL TALE OF LOVE, LOSS AND DESPERATION.

A PRITISH NANDY COMMUNICATIONS CLASSIC

THE
STORY
OF
A
FAMILY
LOVING
MAN
WHO
IS
FORCED
TO
LIVE
ALONE

यादें
یادیں

AJANTA ARTS'

Yaadein

comic Capers

While Bollywood apologists have always maintained that there is a strong comic tradition in Hindi cinema, its clear-eyed critics acknowledge very few true comedies. This is simply because the greats of Bollywood did not really bother too much about them.

When communal harmony had to be emphasized, when socialism had to be explained, when the nation was to be built in a way that would keep financiers happy too, comedy was probably seen as something a trifle frivolous. Perhaps they agreed with cartoonist and satirist OV Vijayan who called laughter a luxury in a nation as riddled by poverty and injustice as ours. Still, there are few films so sullen that they do not allow for some scenes meant to induce laughter.

Despite the ubiquity of comic relief, the figure of the Bollywood comic was never paid too much attention. He was borrowed from other traditions – folk theatre, Bombay's Parsi theatre, circus acts involving dwarfs and fat ladies – without any major modifications. Thus the broad gestures and gross overacting that would carry to the cheap seats were brought straight to the screen.

Every aspect of the comic had to be pointedly funny: his clothes were infantile, his speech was mannered, his face mobile to the point of contortion, his head was bald or he was without teeth. The comic could never throw away a line; each one had to be punched in and often underlined with illustrative gestures. And as if to make sure the audience knew that the fat man wearing brilliant pink shorts and a cap with a feather stuck in it was a comic, the background score would give him a signature two-bar entry.

The tradition of the *vidhushak* or decadent Brahmin, whose comic effects were produced by a surface absurdity that masked deeper social comment, had been jettisoned. However, as the poster of *Raja Saab* (1969, Suraj Prakash) shows, certain elements of his persona such as the lock of hair he sported, could still be used as a mnemonic. The lock of hair on Shashi Kapoor's head above is the same as that worn by Brahmins.

It was only when a few comedians like IS Johar, OP Ralhan and Mehmood achieved some measure of success at the box office and could headline their own productions, that the comic was briefly retrieved from pathetic idiocy. One of these movies was *Mera Naam Johar* (1968, Sarankant), which played on the title *Mera Naam Joker* (1969, Raj Kapoor), the famous film made by the much more saleable Raj Kapoor who used humour to point out the wrongs of society. However, Raj Kapoor's films belong more clearly to the genre of the social. His funniest, *Shree 420* and *Awaara*, for instance, were marked by their concerns for the small man as represented by Raju, the Indian version of Charlie Chaplin. Kapoor wanted to carve out some cinematic space for a sentimental portrait of India's little guy, the humble but honest cog in the wheel. Guru Dutt too made the witty *Mr & Mrs 55*, though he is better remembered as the poet of the poor, the tormented loser turning his face against the world.

Posters for comedies always underlined the ridiculous. They used non-standard fonts for the lettering; caricatures were common as were strange expressions, generally of surprise. Not much attention was paid by the artists to these posters. But that might be because the comedy has spent almost all its life, save the last ten years, as a B-grade film. David Dhawan had his moment in the sun with a series of hits with the dancing comic star Govinda (*Aankhen* in 1993, *Coolie No 1* in 1995), but they were situational comedies that relied heavily on misogyny and innuendo. Only recently has the comedy ascended a few rungs of the ladder in the hands of directors like Priyadarshan (*Hera Pheri* in 2000, *Bhool Bhulaiyya* in 2007), Dibakar Banerjee (*Khosla Ka Ghosla* in 2007) and Anees Bazmi (*No Entry* in 2005, *Welcome* in 2007), and begun to attract both bigger stars and budgets.

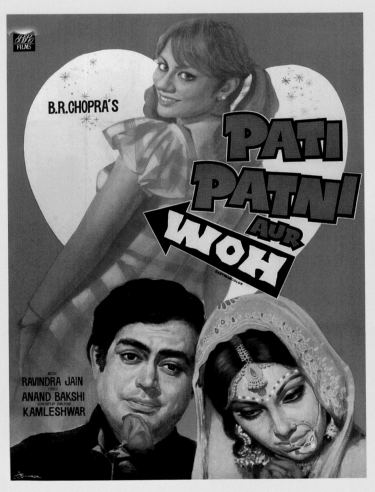

CRIME

There were five Sikh friends in the Punjab who didn't read English but they saw the poster of a film, *Chupke Chupke* – the poster had a picture of Amitabh Bachchan and Dharmendra and that was enough. These five friends went in to see the film. But as you know, *Chupke Chupke* is a comedy. The audience came out disappointed and dejected. One of the friends complained that there wasn't a single fist fight, wrestling or jostling scene in this film. Another friend asked, 'What is the name of the film director?' The fellow who could read a little saw the poster and said, 'The director is someone called Rishki Pushki Mukherjee! [laughs loudly]. This director has two lions in his movie and doesn't do anything with them.' Fighting is a must for audiences in the North and as Dharmendra and Amitabh Bachchan have the image of action heroes, how can the audience accept seeing them without action?

– Mahendra Varma, stunt director

From BOLLYWOOD: THE INDIAN CINEMA STORY by Nasreen Munni Kabir

Anton Chekhov is said to have laid down the law: "If in the first act you have hung a pistol on the wall, then in the following one it should be fired. Otherwise don't put it there." In the case of Bollywood films, that could read: If a pistol or other firearm shows up on the poster, it must go off in the film. Or one might even go as far as to say: If a certain actor shows up in the poster of a film, fists must fly, guns must go off and blood must flow copiously or the audience will go away disappointed.

After sound was introduced in cinema, almost all Hindi films had some kind of fight scene thrown in. However, these scenes generally gave cinematic expression to the idea of the struggle between good and evil. If this sounds moralistic, one should remember that most Hindi films were configured as morality plays. They made concrete the abstract, and the hero's participation in them was only symbolic.

When film noir arrived, things began to change somewhat. *Kismet* (1943, Gyan Mukherjee) was an early harbinger of the noir film. It starred Ashok Kumar and Devika Rani, and ran for three years at a theatre in Kolkata. According to PK Nair, the Director of the National Film Archives of India, it was the first film to suggest another kind of hero.

Before *Kismet*... hit the jackpot at the box office, screen heroes of the early Bombay Talkies film were less 'heroic': sympathetic and understanding no doubt, but generally whitewashed and virtuous. The debonair golden-hearted pickpocket of *Kismet* demonstrated that the screen's leading characters could even be grey!

From ASHOK KUMAR: GREEN TO EVERGREEN edited by Rani Burra for the

International Film Festival of India, 1990

Kismet might be considered an early example of a crime film – its central protagonist is a thief and it is his theft of a necklace that precipitates events. It was only in the 1950s that Bollywood began to develop the outlines of its own version of noir. The chiaroscuro of Hollywood, its sharp shadows and striking light effects, were turned to good use in a cinema that enjoyed painting in swathes of black and white. The posters from this era routinely feature dark silhouettes, perhaps also a way of suggesting that the figure so concealed was of ambiguous moral standing. When colour was used, the overwhelming hues were red (blood) and black (night/evil). In the posters in this section, you can see how this darkness is used to indicate any number of possibilities: in *Don* (2006, Farhan Akhtar) it is used to suggest the mystery surrounding the identity of a criminal; in *Johnny Gaddaar* (2007, Sriram Raghavan) for the evil that arises from the immoral pursuit of money; in *Teesri Manzil* (1966, Vijay Anand) the blacks suggest the mysterious death of a young woman who has committed suicide and for whom vengeance is sought.

Noir has always demanded a male protagonist whose exploits we would follow as he worked his way through the urban labyrinth. The central character of the film, often the narrator, had to be a creature of the city, aware of the dangers it represented but with the insouciance to keep trying the patience of the beast. Of the three male stars who dominated the marquee in those days, Raj Kapoor could not play the noir hero. He was the male version of an ingénue, still starry-eyed from the village, himself a victim of the city's machinations in *Shree 420* (1955, Raj Kapoor). Dilip Kumar had established himself as the man with the wound. In film after film, love would fail him since he brought to it an idealized romanticism. It was therefore Dev Anand who took over the space. Starting with *Taxi Driver* (1954, Chetan Anand), Anand played a series of urban and urbane heroes. In the *Johny Mera Naam* (1970, Vijay Anand) poster, we see him emerge from darkness, which could be a wall, an alley or simply the night. His clothes define the western influences at work on him – and by extension on all that was wrong with the city. Popular discourse in India pitted the city against the village.

Then, as now, an overwhelming majority of the Indian population lived in villages. The village was therefore constructed as a source of purity and innocence. The city was a locus of danger; it was presented, ahistorically, as a western invention. In the 1950s, India went through a huge feeling of ambivalence to the West and to its products. The city was seen as alluring in that it held out the promise of money, anonymity and independence. But it was also a moral threat as much as a physical one. The threat of physical harm emanated from the goons and the gangs; the attack on the hero's moral fibre from the woman in the shadows. This person was clearly not the heroine of the film. It was the vamp, the dancing girl, invariably presented as a Christian with a name like Rosie, Lily or Mary. She was often played by the dancing star Helen who hoofed it through an incredible three decades of cinema.

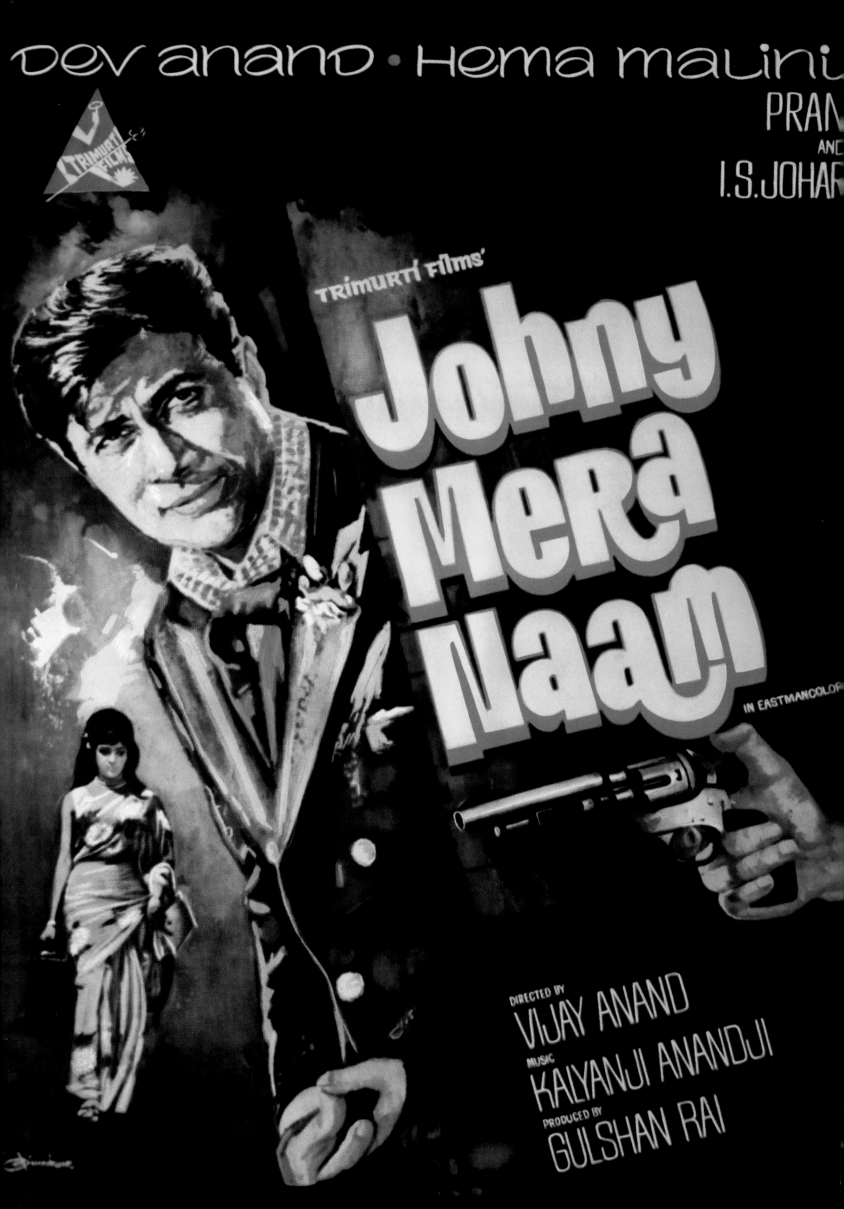

Both the male and female central protagonists in western noir were not repositories of moral wisdom. The men were presented as opportunists or the victims of desperate women. The women might need rescuing but it was clear that they shared the city's disregard for the morality of the means by which they sought their ends.

By contrast, the Indian film heroine of the late 1950s and 1960s might have been in the city but was certainly not of it. She held herself aloof from the moral turpitude around her. She represented another moral pole to the attractions of the metropolis. If she worked, it was at some "noble profession" such as teaching. In *Kala Bazaar* (1960, Chetan Anand), Alka (Waheeda Rehman) is the kind of woman who tears up cinema tickets bought at black-market prices. It is to win her love that Raghuveer (Dev Anand) teaches himself to read, rejects the easy money of the streets and finally dissolves his gang of black-market ticket sellers. In *House No 44* (1955, MK Burman), Ashok (Dev Anand) tells Nimmo (Kalpana Kartik) that he needs her support to pursue honesty as an ideal. He can only do this by leaving the gang for which he has been working. Observe that even the poster of *Johny Mera Naam* offers us the same belief system by investing it in the clothes that the characters wear. The male protagonist is wearing western clothes; his name, Johny, has a western ring to it. Again, by contrast, the woman is wearing a sari. She seems a source of light in the frame, the flare of which rises from behind her and is magnified in the light colour of her sari. When darkness threatens to overcome our hero, it is the heroine who is a beacon of light. If this does not seem like a departure from Hollywood noir, imagine Robert Mitchum asking Veronica Lake's help in turning over a new leaf.

Noir in India differed from film noir in the West in another significant way: the location of the moral centre of the film. Western noir rejected the idea of morality in favour of ethics. The ethical code was located in the hero and it was made clear, again and again, that it was a code of his own creation and he would apply it, and his gun, to achieve his ends. In India, few films of the 1950s and 1960s would try to escape the vice of morality. The guilty were always punished, the innocent set free and justice was served. If the hero had transgressed the moral order, he went to jail and came out of it, one dissolve or wipe later, ready to take his place in society again.

In the early 1960s the entry of heroines like Asha Parekh, Babita and Rajshree, and of several trained dancers from the South of the country, turned the Hindi film heroine from a goddess in a white sari into a spirited young woman who could dance and flirt. Murder mysteries became more common since they allowed for much play between notions of innocence and guilt, and allowed the hero and the heroine to visit suspect areas such as hotels and nightclubs in search of the truth. Our cover girl Sharmila Tagore holds her gun with a coquettish, almost flirtatious, air. She is aware, it would seem, of the multiple psycho-sexual meanings of the gun.

Then, in 1973, Prakash Mehra's *Zanjeer* was released and the notion of violence changed forever. Amitabh Bachchan brought the Angry Young Man to the screen, playing Vijay, a young cop who turns vigilante in search of his parents' murderers. The film was a turning point in the on-screen depiction of violence. Earlier fights had not sought to involve the audience. They arrived at a point in the film where the resolution was clearly in sight. Here, every plot point was anointed with blood. Each blow was dealt with a certain visceral intensity. The anger spilling out of Bachchan redefined the way in which heroes would fight. Gone was the limp-wristed stylization of Dev Anand or the comical physicality of Shammi Kapoor. This was a violence of the mind, as intense in motion as in speech.

The posters accordingly reinvented the male form. Before, the hero was seen in romantic or contemplative postures; now he was poised for violence. In *Yaadon Ki Zanjeer* (1984, Shibu Mitra), for instance, we see no women in the poster. The men are ready to act, and act violently. A pistol is aimed out of the frame of the poster, pointed at the viewer. In the *Mastan Dada* (1977, Satyen Bose) poster, a red eye brings to mind Raudra Shiva or the God of Destruction in a rage. The hero and heroine run, but flight seems futile. They are under surveillance.

The next film to make such an impact was *Deewaar* (1975, Yash Chopra). Here, Bachchan played Vijay again, a young man who has been tattooed with his father's infamy. Bearing the words "*Mera baap chor hai*" (My father is a thief) on his forearm, Vijay grows up an atheist and soon joins the underworld. The first fight, staged in a warehouse, has become a cinema classic. When it played in theatres, men in the audience flinched as the blows fell, their bodies tensed as the hero prepared to attack. In the same year, another landmark film, *Sholay*, was released. Director Shekhar Kapur once said, "Hindi cinema can be divided into two eras: Before *Sholay* and After *Sholay*." It is also possible to say that director Ramesh Sippy, assisted by scriptwriters Salim Khan and Javed Akhtar, rewrote the villain when they crafted the role of Gabbar Singh. Amjad Khan brought a new savagery to the role of a dacoit but it was the suggestion of violence that released the power of audience imagination: the killing of a fly as a metaphor for the extinguishing of a human life; the sound of a locomotive exhaust replacing the shot that will kill a child; the creak of an empty swing to suggest the annihilation of a family. Gabbar Singh made it necessary for the screenwriter to work at producing not just a powerful hero figure but also a credible antagonist for him.

Oddly, it was Shekhar Kapur who gave us a villain to remember: Mogambo (Amrish Puri) in *Mr India* (1987). Mogambo offers his henchmen the ultimate Hobson's choice: either they leap into a pool full of pink acid which reduces them immediately to skeletons or else. (The alternative is obviously so horrible that all of them choose the pool, turning the villain's name into a metaphor for evil.) But it is evident in Mogambo's over-the-top lair and in

Anupam Kher's Dr Michael Dang in *Karma* (1986, Subhash Ghai) that the villain had reached such a nadir of villainy, he could only turn into a camp version of himself. Both Mogambo and Dr Dang have something of the operatic villain, who would now share space on the poster with the lead pair.

This violence also changed the way women were portrayed. The girl had now grown up. She was allowed to bare her arms. Whenever a woman in a poster points a gun, there is an element of self-consciousness: the phallic symbol has been turned around. An obvious meaning is symbolic castration. But it can also be seen as an expression of penis envy, as an appropriation of masculinity, or even as part of an ancient stereotyping where the frisson arises out of the disjunction between the way a woman is seen (non-violent and passive) and the manifest destiny of a gun. *Putli Bai* (1972, Ashok Roy) is an obvious example of a film from a certain tradition in which an early injustice turns a woman into a dacoit. In most posters for films of this sub-genre, the woman is shown seated on a horse (another phallic symbol) and brandishing a gun. The poster invites us to see her as a modern version of Kali, a goddess combining the powers of the triumvirate of gods (Vishnu, Shiva and Brahma), a goddess brought to earth to fight injustice. The heroine on the horse is generally portrayed in the film as unconquerable until she is "gentled" by love. This is also what happens to Kali, who is about to destroy the earth when her husband, Shiva, throws himself in her path and stops her. The *Pratighaat* poster (1987, N Chandra) makes this equation clearer. The heroine has an axe in her hands. The blood on it tells us that she hasn't come from cutting down a tree.

Just when everyone thought the violent film couldn't get any more violent, along came *Satya* (1998, Ram Gopal Varma) which opened the doors for another wave of blood, gore and spit. Here were gunmen in ordinary clothes, underworld bosses who lived in housing societies and a hero (JD Chakravarthy) whose face had the ordinariness of the boy next door. The poster too was crafted as if Satya was rising from or descending into the Stygian depths of Mumbai's underworld. Through the 1970s and 1980s, the action film constituted a genre known as the "dishoom-dishoom film", an onomatopoeic name for the soundtrack's embellishment of every screen punch. *Satya* replaced those sounds with the bass whoomp of a silenced revolver being fired or the staccato laughter of a machine gun. The old Urdu-Hindustani mix has been replaced with street lingo, an argot called Tapori, which means both the street goon and the language he speaks. Where the crime film acted as a moral lesson, it is now an amoral tale in which no one knows who will win. In many of his films, producer and director Varma seeks to position his audience on the side of the vigilante or the man who operates outside the law. Only a very few films buck this trend. *Bluffmaster* (2005, Rohan Sippy) is one exception offering a light-hearted caper instead of gore-splashed gang wars. This has continued through to films like *Johnny Gaddaar* where the central character seems motivated only by the love of money. Western noir's amorality may finally have arrived in India.

GURU DUTT · SHYAMA · JOHNNY WALKER & SHAKILA
GURU DUTT FILM'S
AAR PAAR
PRODUCER & DIRECTOR
GURU DUTT
MUSIC
O.P. NAYYAR
DIALOGUE
ABRAR ALVI
आर पार

NIGARISTAN (INDIA) FILMS PRESENT
देहली जंक्शन

DELHI JUNCTION

SHAKILA · AJIT · NISHI AND PRAN

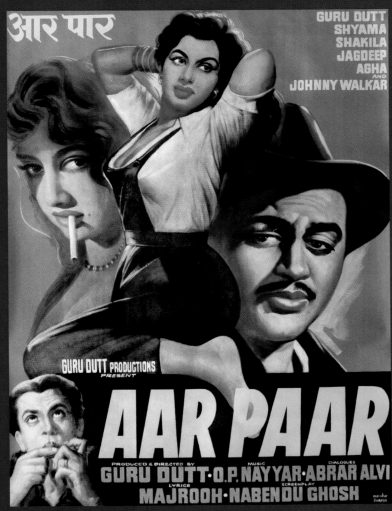

आर पार

GURU DUTT
SHYAMA
SHAKILA
JAGDEEP
AGHA
AND
JOHNNY WALKAR

GURU DUTT PRODUCTIONS PRESENT

AAR PAAR

PRODUCED & DIRECTED BY   MUSIC   DIALOGUES
GURU DUTT · O.P. NAY YAR · ABRAR ALVI
LYRICS   SCREENPLAY
MAJROOH · NABENDU GHOSH

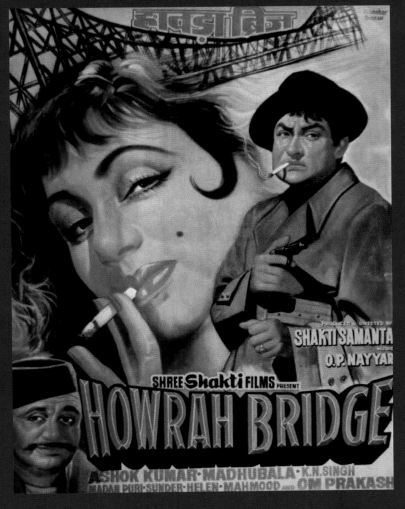

हावड़ा ब्रिज

PRODUCED & DIRECTED BY
SHAKTI SAMANTA
MUSIC
O.P. NAY YAR

SHREE Shakti FILMS PRESENT

HOWRAH BRIDGE

ASHOK KUMAR · MADHUBALA · K.N. SINGH
MADAN PURI · SUNDER · HELEN · MAHMOOD AND OM PRAKASH

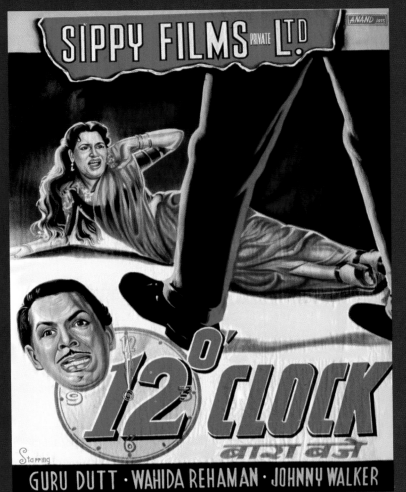

SIPPY FILMS PRIVATE LTD.

ANAND 2015

Starring

12 O' CLOCK
बारह बजे

GURU DUTT · WAHIDA REHAMAN · JOHNNY WALKER

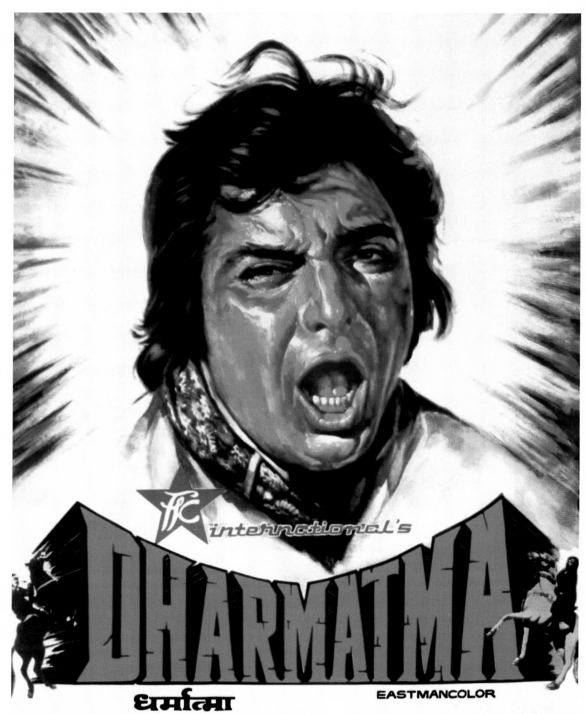

NWP New World Picture
ALA SINHA
SWAJEET
HNY WALKER
Jaal
EASTMANCOLOR
जाल
جال
DIRECTED BY
MONI BHATTACHARJEE
MUSIC
LAXMIKANT PYARELAL
PRODUCED BY
A.R.KHAN . B.R.PACHISIA

NAVKETAN'S

Jewel Thief

EASTMANCOLOR

PRODUCED BY
DEV ANAND
DIRECTED BY
VIJAY ANAND
MUSIC
S. D. BURMAN

جیول تھیف

जीयूल थीप

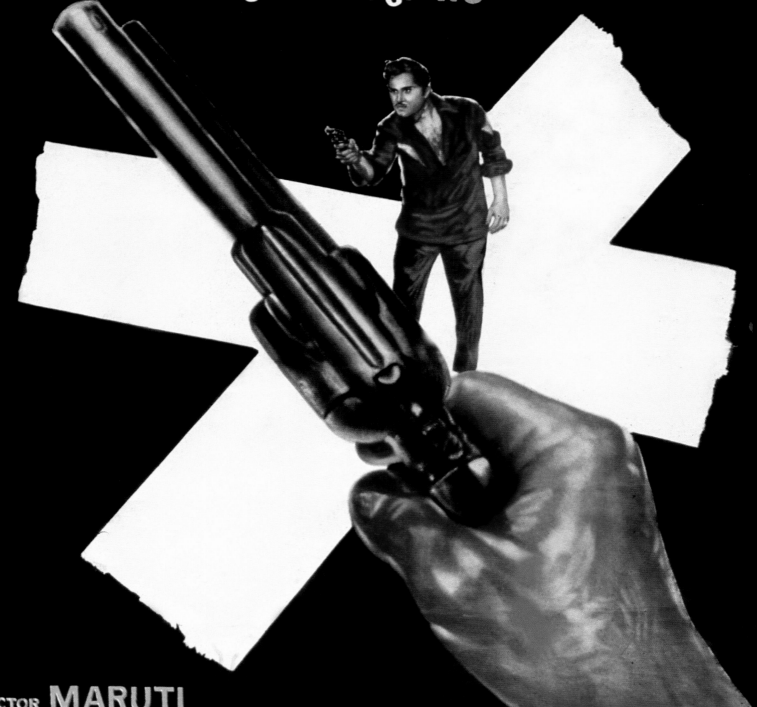

श्रीदास दामानी प्रस्तुतकरतेहैं
एस. श्रीवास्तवजीका

कहीं आर कहीं पार

Kahin AAR Kahin PAAR
in GEVACOLOR

दिग्दर्शक मारुती
संगीत गणेश

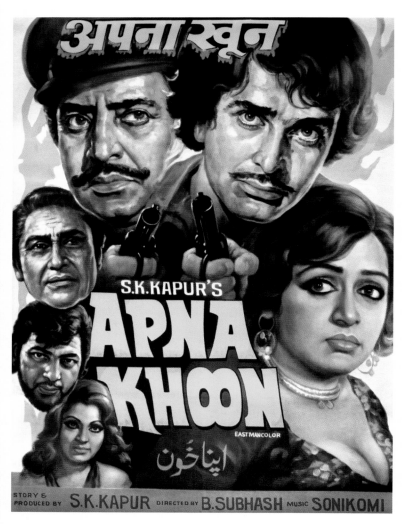

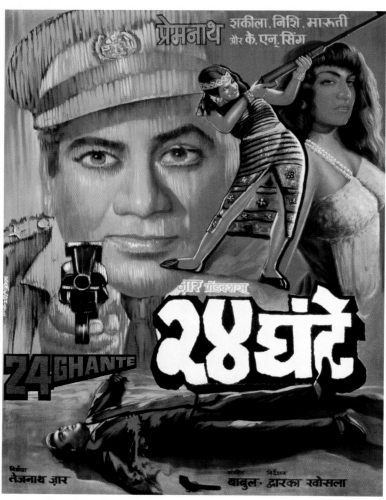

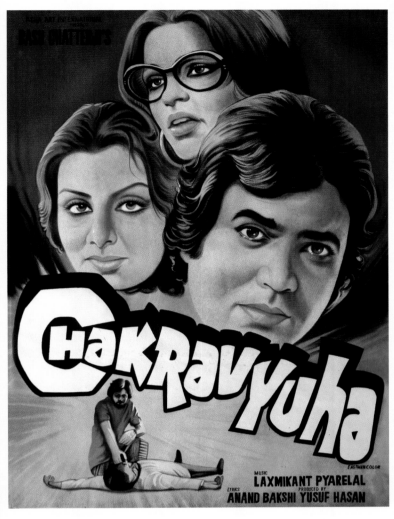

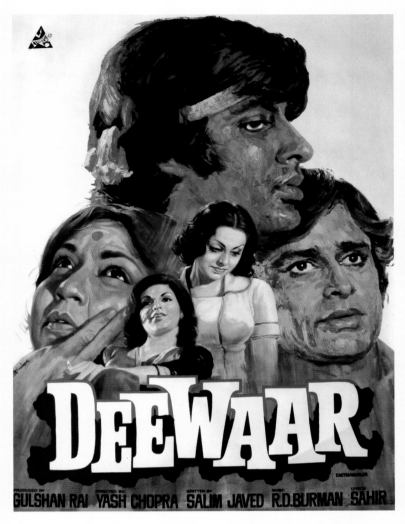

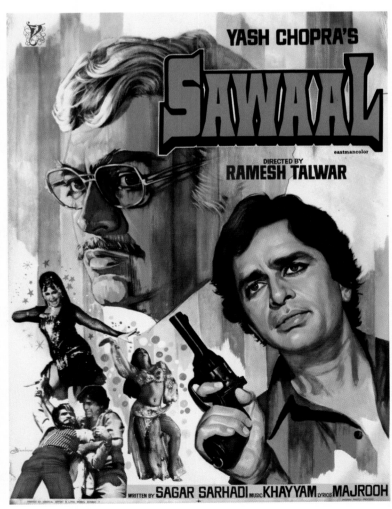

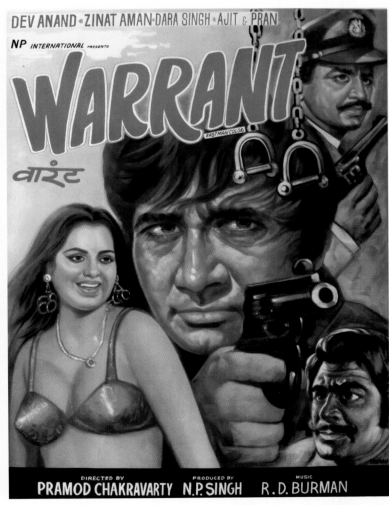

NASIR HUSAIN FILMS *PRESENT*

SHAMMI KAPOOR
ASHA PAREKH

Teesri Manzil

EASTMANCOLOR

WRITTEN & PRODUCED BY
NASIR HUSAIN
DIRECTED BY
VIJAY ANAND
MUSIC
R.D. BURMAN
LYRICS
MAJROOH

तीसरी मंझिल
تیسری منزل

ASSOCIATED FILMS & FINANCE CORPORATION
presents

eastmancolor

the **GREAT**
GAMBLER

eastmancolor

DIRECTED BY
SHAKTI SAMANTA
C.V.K. SHASTRY

MUSIC **R.D. BURMAN** LYRICS **ANAND BAKSHI** PRODUCED BY: **C.V.K. SHASTRY**

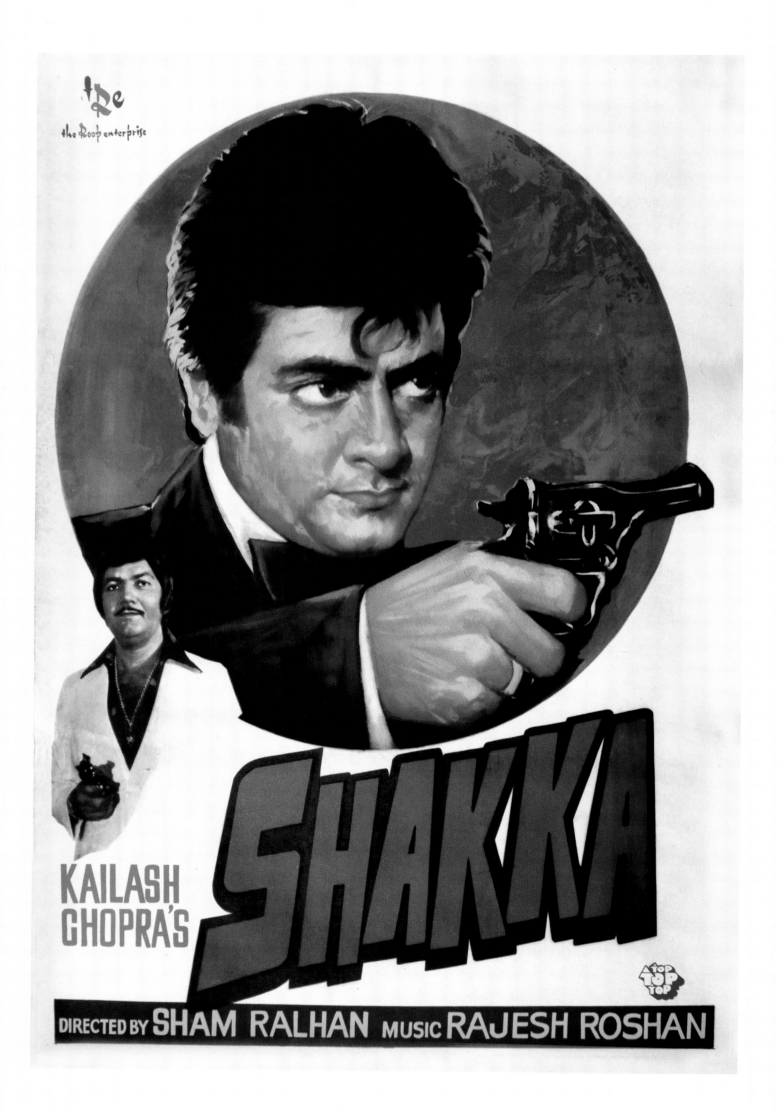

DOONDY PRESENTS
BHARATI INTERNATIONAL'S
RAKSHA
CAMERA & DIRECTED BY
RAVEE NAGAICH
MUSIC
R.D.BURMAN
LYRICS
ANAND BAKSHI
PRODUCED BY
P.MALLIKHARJUNA RAO

GEMINI
presents

a N.N. SIPPY PRODUCTIO[N]

Shatranj

in EASTMANCOLO[R]

DIRECTION
S.S. VASAN · **SHANKER** MUSIC **JAIKISHAN** · **K.H. KAPADIA** PHOTOGRAPHY

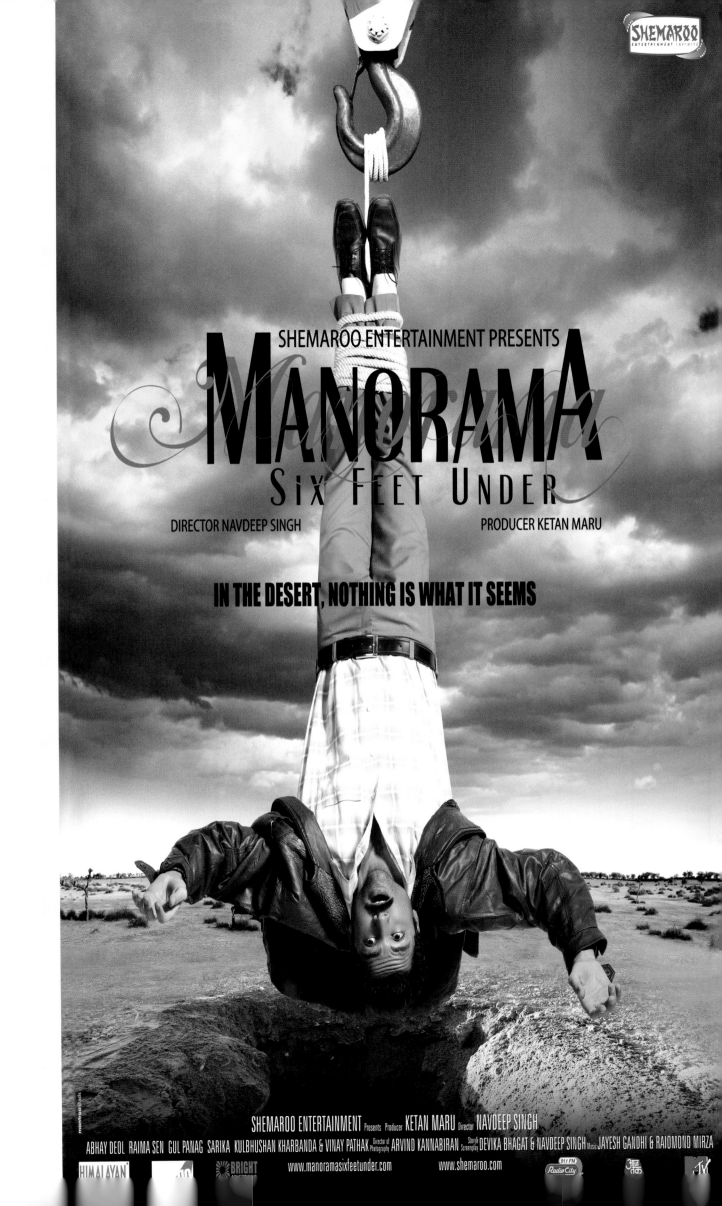

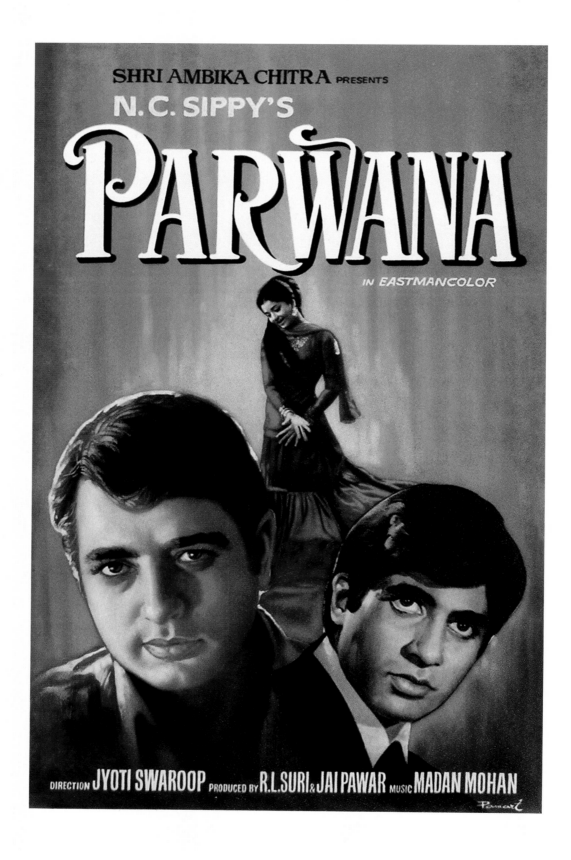

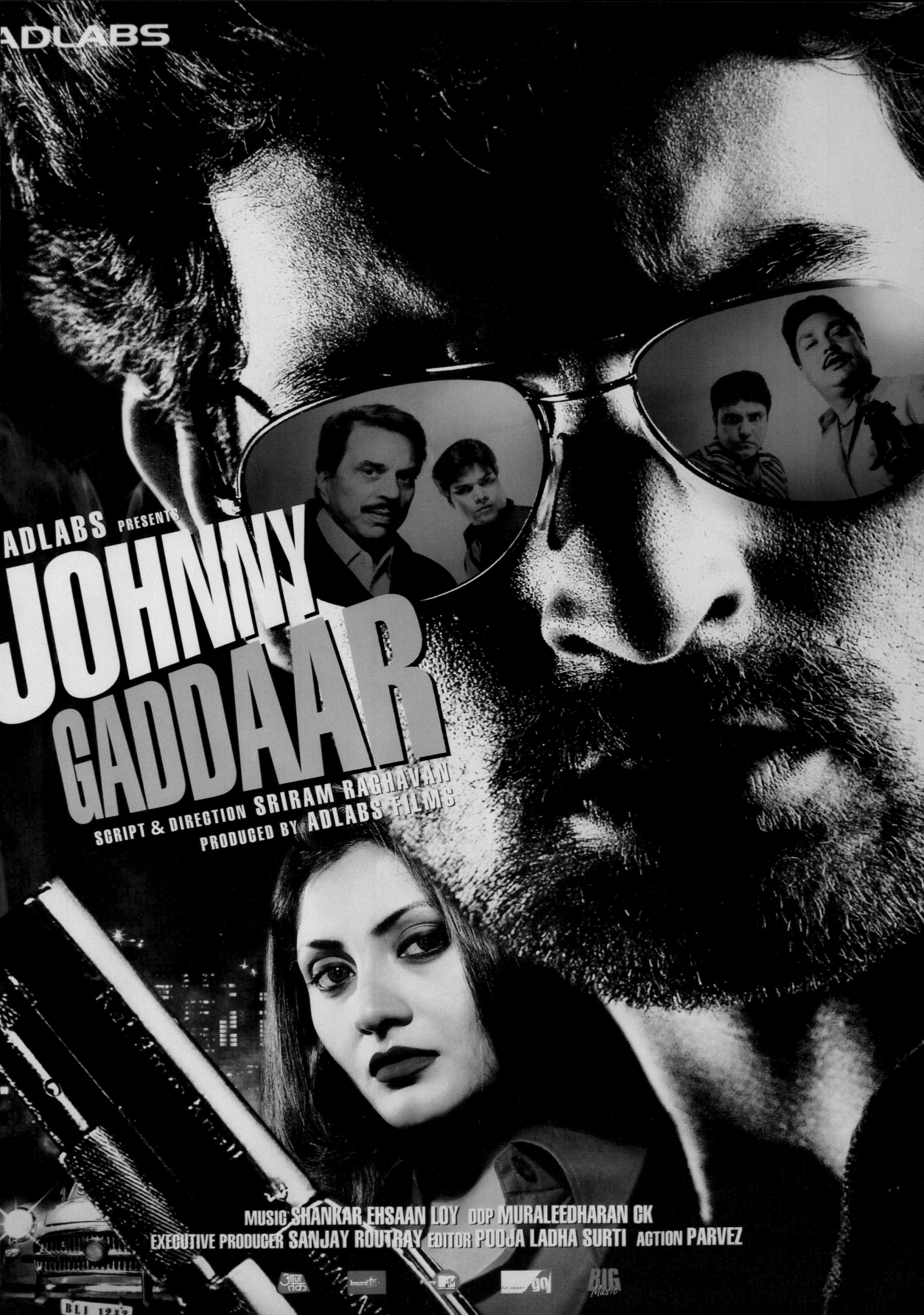
ADLABS
ADLABS PRESENTS
JOHNNY GADDAAR
SCRIPT & DIRECTION SRIRAM RAGHAVAN
PRODUCED BY ADLABS FILMS
MUSIC SHANKAR EHSAAN LOY DOP MURALEEDHARAN CK
EXECUTIVE PRODUCER SANJAY ROUTRAY EDITOR POOJA LADHA SURTI ACTION PARVEZ
BIG Music

A FILM BY FARHAN AKHTAR

DON

PRODUCED BY RITESH SIDHWANI

Bollywood Posters

PRODUCER: **ADITYA CHOPRA**
LYRICS: **SAMEER**

CHILL BILL

With Joseph Wirsching behind the camera and Kamal Amrohi as director, the horror film genre got off to a flying start with the haunting *Mahal* (1949). Sadly, that high standard was not to be maintained and the genre soon became associated with B-grade movies intent on killing starlets and spilling much blood on-screen, all of which was lavishly displayed on the poster. The horror film poster is thus an invitation into one's own subconscious.

Bollywood's flirtation with the occult can be examined along three axes. There is the reincarnation drama, where a pair of lovers dies before they can marry or consummate their love. They are reborn and then seek each other out again. The Bengali auteur Ritwick Ghatak can be said to have written one of the first and still most beautifully mounted of these, *Madhumati* (1958, Bimal Roy), but the theme has been revisited in later productions such as *Milan* (1967, A Subba Rao), *Karz* (1980, Subhash Ghai), *Kudrat* (1981, Chetan Anand) and recently *Om Shanti Om* (2007, Farah Khan).

The second kind is the mock horror film where it seems as if something supernatural is going on but this is eventually revealed to be the doing of someone human for some ordinary human end, such as driving an heiress mad and getting her money or bringing someone to justice as happens in *Gumnaam* (1965, Raja Nawathe), *Ek Nanhi Munni Ladki Thi* (1970, Vishram Bedekar) and *Woh Kaun Thi?* (1964, Raj Khosla).

The third type is the genuine horror film which calls for a suspension of disbelief and a willingness to accept that there are such things as vampires, that locked doors in ancient homes should not be forced open and that a young woman in a revealing nightgown will step out of her bedroom to follow a beacon or other unearthly will o' the wisp into a cemetery. A small production house called the Ramsays generally made these films. FU Ramsay headed the operation and every film seemed to incorporate the skills of many members of the family. Tulsi and Shyam Ramsay were credited with direction. *Saamri* (1985), now a cult film for its eponymous central character who, bizarrely, is part vampire and part social reformer, offers a bouquet of Ramsays. Shyam Ramsay edited the film, Kiran Ramsay handled sound, the associate director was Arjun Ramsay who also wrote the screenplay, the photographer was Gangu Ramsay and Kanta Ramsay was the producer. In *Aakhri Cheekh* (1991), Anita Ramsay is credited as the office assistant; *Shaitaani Ilaaka* (1990) was produced by Reshma Ramsay while the costume designer is Kavita Ramsay. *Mahakaal* (1993) introduces us to assistant directors Sunil, Deepak, Pappu and Shashi Ramsay but Chander Ramsay directs the film. *Bandh Darwaza* (1990) has Anjali Ramsay… no doubt there are others who contributed in different ways.

The classic Ramsay film works with a disruption in the social order. A car, the symbol of modernity, brings a group of young people to an old house. If the car breaks down on a stormy night, the failure of the rational is made even more explicit. The young people do what they are told not to do: enter a vault, visit a cemetery or open a book. The consequences are horrific. Some minor characters pay with their lives. The situation is saved only when a tantrik holy man steps in and fights fire with fire. The message is clear. Though evil has been defeated and the chastened lead pair may now return to the city and the normal world, it is defeated by an equally antediluvian force of good alone, one that bases itself on religious adherence.

It is with the arrival of Ram Gopal Varma's *Raat* (1992) that the horror film was invested with some measure of cinematic finesse. With a new breed of such directors coming into its own in Bollywood, we are likely to see slicker films made with terrifying posters that really do send shivers down the spine, rather than the monsters we see here which make us merely chuckle at their clumsy waxen faces.

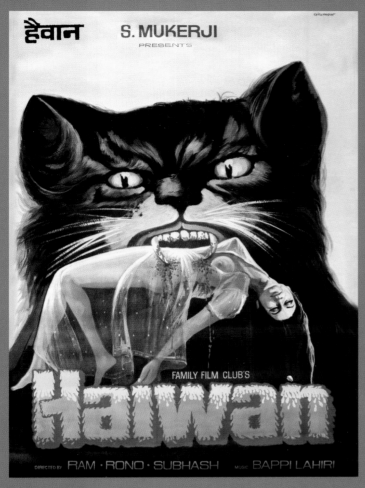

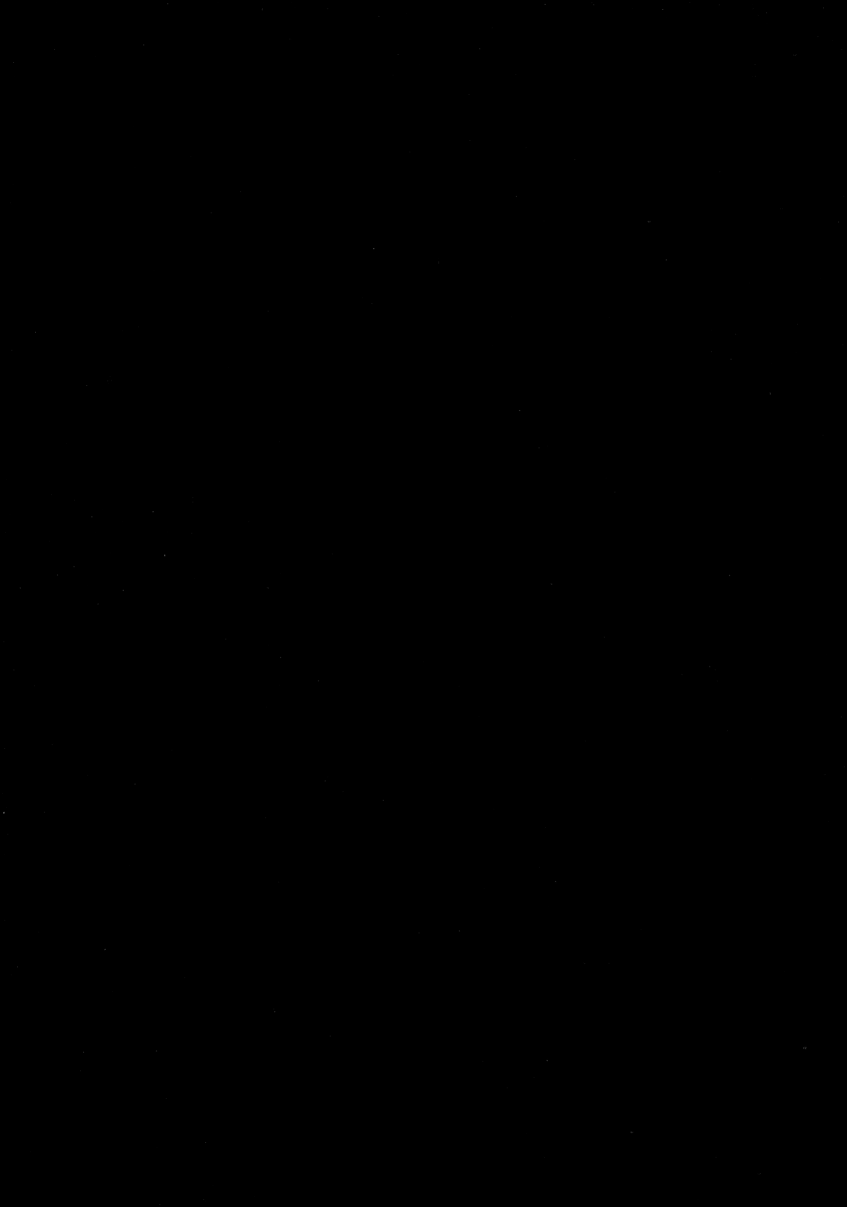

HISTORY

There are some critics who think that a historical film is actually about history. Many reviews carp about inconsistent details: the clothes worn were not faithful to the times, the speech patterns were too modern, the cars on the roads were not the kind that were driven in that age, an over as a measure of the number of balls bowled in cricket did not consist of six balls in the 19th century, and so on.

As Bollywood begins its inevitable, and some might say welcome, progress towards the Hollywood notion of cinematic realism, it might be a good time to remind ourselves that historical films are not made to represent the past; instead they try to influence the present by creating the past. When *Naya Daur* (1957, BR Chopra) was made, it was not about whether a horse carriage could actually race a bus, but about a struggle for the kind of India we would want. (Or, more interestingly, the kind of India we would like to be seen to want.) When Shankar (Dilip Kumar) drives his horse-drawn *tonga* to victory, he reasserts some fundamental notions about India.

Under the rubric of the historical we have included films set in the non-recent past, those that offered a cinematic vision of the building of the Indian nation. Many of these films have been fantastically successful at the box office. The 20 highest earners of Hindi cinema include at least six films that concern themselves with themes that directly affect the nation. *Mughal-e-Azam* (1957, K Asif) begins with the spirit of India speaking directly to the audience, before introducing us to Emperor Akbar. *Mother India* (1957, Mehboob Khan) practically created an equation between the Nation State and Radha (Nargis), the protagonist who sacrifices her family for her duty. *Kranti* (1981, Manoj Kumar) was a Bollywood version of the events of the First War of Indian Independence in 1857. *Roti Kapda aur Makaan* (1974, Manoj Kumar) addressed problems of society such as the need for food, clothing and shelter, and the difficulty the middle class and the poor faced to get these basics in an unjust society. *Lage Raho Munnabhai* (2006, Raju Hirani) had Mahatma Gandhi reform an urban gangster and turn him to the path of non-violent protest. *Naya Daur* deals with the notion of the self-sufficient village and the incursion of modernity with the arrival of a bus service. *Gadar: Ek Prem Katha* (2001, Anil Sharma) deals with the India-Pakistan divide through the story of Tara (Sunny Deol), a Sikh boy who falls in love with Sakina (Amisha Patel), a Muslim girl. They marry but when she goes back to see her family, they try to annul the marriage. Tara follows her and is asked to change his religion, settle in Pakistan and denounce India to win her back. His decisions in these matters offer a new hierarchy of passion.

It becomes clear from this roll of honour that Bollywood has always played an important role in the shaping of the idea of the nation. "*Yeh desh hai veer jawaanon ka*" (Our land is a land of brave soldiers) went a popular and rousing song from *Naya Daur*. Thus several films were made around the real-life character of Bhagat Singh, the early

20th-century revolutionary hanged for killing a police officer who had shot another freedom fighter. In 1954 came *Shaheed-E-Azam Bhagat Singh* (Jagdish Gautam). This was followed by *Shaheed Bhagat Singh* (1963, KN Bansal), *Shaheed* (1965, S Ram Sharma) and, finally, *The Legend of Bhagat Singh* (2002, Raj Kumar Santoshi). The year 2002 was good for India's most famous martyr. The Indian news portal, rediff.com, reported that five films were being made on Bhagat Singh. Some of these may never have been finished or released, but the numbers show a shift from *ahimsa* (the Gandhian ideal of non-violence) to the freedom fighter with a gun in his hand.

The image here must seem at odds with the project of nationalism in its emphasis on *swadeshi*, or the use of goods produced in India by Indians for Indians, symbolized in Mahatma Gandhi's *charkha*, or spinning wheel, with which he hoped to fight British economic colonialism and return India to its prelapsarian past of idyllic self-contained villages. In contrast to most freedom fighters shown wearing Indian clothes, Bhagat Singh wore a hat, otherwise routinely used to distinguish the "England-returned" (read, westernized) young man. We have only a few images of Bhagat Singh from which an entire iconography had to be drawn. Just as medieval painters of Christian saints did not bother with differentiating faces and concentrated on symbols with which the faithful could identify the saints, the poster makers of India used certain strategic elements to create different freedom fighters. Bhagat Singh's image was drawn from a picture that appeared in the Lahore edition of *The Tribune* on the day after his execution. In this photograph, taken in a studio at Chandni Chowk in Delhi, he is wearing a hat of Italian make. In the hands of the artists who drew him for the lurid charts that formed a part of Indian pedagogical methods, the hat steadily morphed into a fedora.

The *Rang De Basanti* (2006, Rakeysh Omprakash Mehra) poster does not use the Bhagat Singh figure, although he looms large in the minds of the film's youthful protagonists, catalysing them from uncaring hedonists to committed citizens. Although the method it suggested was nihilistic and smacked of the vigilantism of the 1970s, the film is said to have caused many young people to rethink their connections with the body politic. Otherwise, all the other posters for the Bhagat Singh films have played with this image.

In a similar manner, the figures of Rani Lakshmibai of Jhansi and Alexander the Great, represented here by his Indianized name Sikandar, have been turned into icons. They are warriors and war is always a challenge to the filmmaker and a thrill for the audience. The promise of spectacle is implicit in a historical poster. Massed armies – which fill the odd corners of the poster – do not just mean a battle. The war scenes indicate that money has been spent and this is often equated with quality. Pre-publicity material speaks of a "cast of thousands" and many filmmakers hire retired army officers or historians to ensure that some measure of authenticity has been retained.

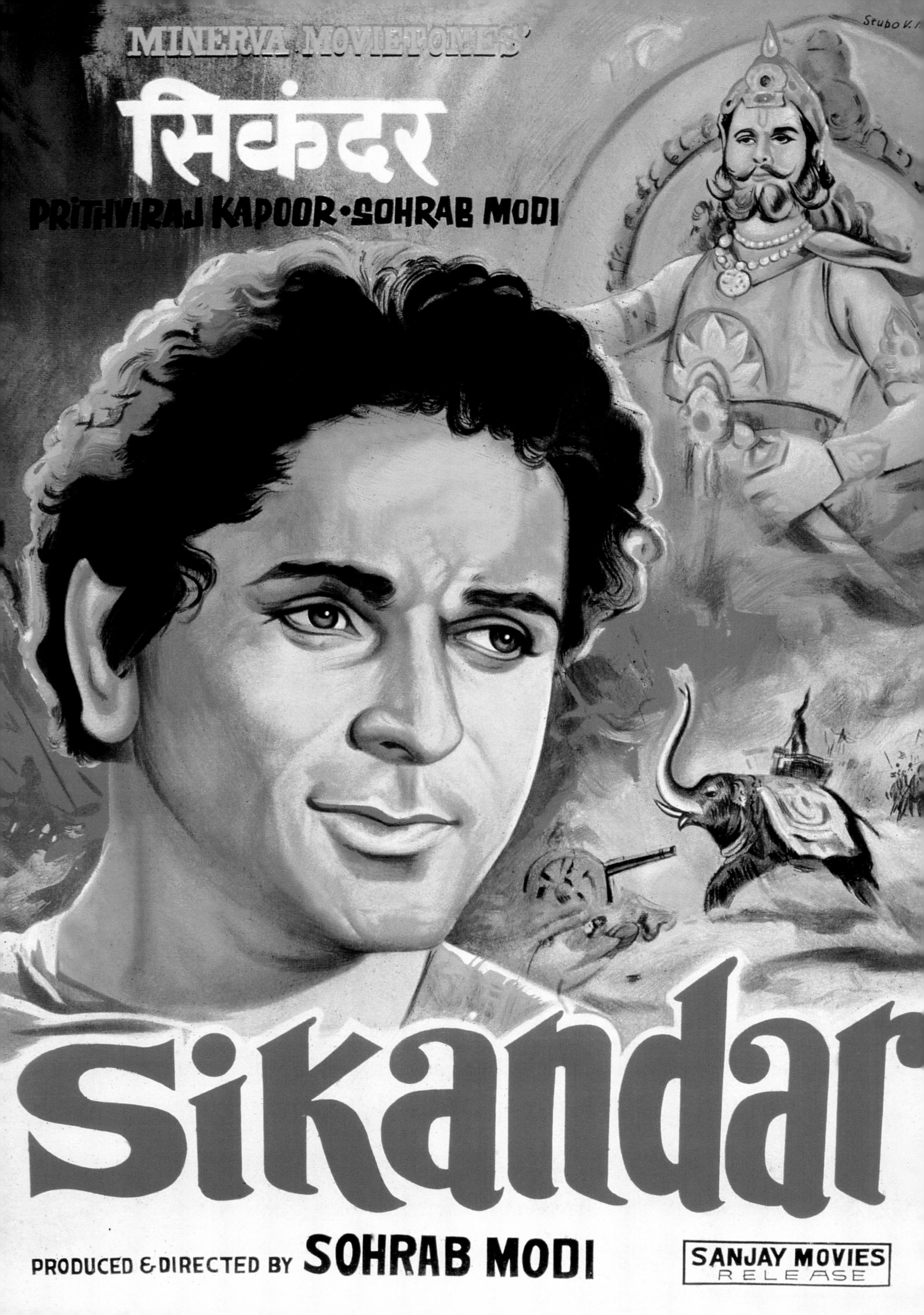
MINERVA MOVIETONES'
सिकंदर
PRITHVIRAJ KAPOOR • SOHRAB MODI
Sikandar
PRODUCED & DIRECTED BY SOHRAB MODI
SANJAY MOVIES
RELEASE

The most successful of these films have used the human element to carry forward both the historical story and message. In the *Mughal-e-Azam* poster, the figures of the lovers cower in a corner while the face of Emperor Akbar (Prithviraj Kapoor) dominates the space. The film uses the legend of the beautiful dancing girl, Anarkali (Madhubala), with whom Emperor Akbar's son Salim (Dilip Kumar) falls in love. The Bollywood anthem, *"Pyaar kiya to darna kya"* (Why should I fear when I have loved?), the only part of this black and white movie to be rendered in colour, enunciates the basic struggle between the anarchic power of love and the call of duty. Duty is a hard taskmaster in India and even the heir apparent to the Indian empire is not exempt. Like most Indian Oedipuses, when Salim revolts, he loses his battle and is sentenced to death. The courtiers plead for mercy but Akbar must show that he is an even-handed king; treason must be punished. Anarkali gives herself up to save his life and promises to withdraw from Salim's life. But, in the end, it is maternal love that saves her and as Anarkali is led away, Akbar reminds her that the pride of the Mughals is in her hands. Though we are led to believe through the film that Salim and Anarkali are truly in love with each other, we know also that they must sacrifice their love so that Salim may keep his tryst with destiny. The *Anarkali* (1953, Nandlal Jaswantlal) poster featured here offers the lovers as sacrificial victims again: the heroine is wrapped in chains while Salim is portrayed as a lover. The emperor is in the chain-mail armour of war. In both films the message is clear. Love must be the sacrifice on the altar of the prince's duty to the state.

But when the imperium of the Mughals can be combined with a love story sanctioned by marriage, an all-time favourite theme emerges. The poster for *Shahjehan* (1946, AR Kardar) takes its cues from what the designer assumed was the Mughal atelier, stylizing the faces until there was no resemblance to the actors. Shahjehan may have had other achievements to his name, but it is for building the Taj Mahal that he is always remembered. If India is home to the Taj Mahal, it is also home to the first female Muslim ruler, Razia Sultan of Delhi. In the thirteenth century, Shams-ud-din Iltutmish of the Mamluk dynasty is said to have nominated his daughter, Razia Sultan, to rule after his death. Razia Sultan only held on to her throne for four years. This did not dissuade Bollywood. In the low-budget *Razia Sultana* (1961, Devendra), the queen is played by Nirupa Roy who spent most of her youth playing goddesses of one kind or another. Later, Hema Malini reprised the role in *Razia Sultan* (1983, Kamal Amrohi). The film was mounted as a spectacular; its publicity material included life-sized dolls seated on swings outside the flagship theatre, Maratha Mandir in central Mumbai. None of which helped; the film failed spectacularly.

Jodhaa Akbar (2008, Ashutosh Gowariker) was clearly a film with a message. Jodhaa was said to be a Hindu Rajput queen; she was married off to Emperor Akbar in an attempt to ease the tensions between the Hindu Rajput states of Rajasthan and the Mughal empire. Gowariker said that he had a message in mind when he chose the subject.

Be it *Lagaan* (a period drama) or *Swades* (a social drama), I have just poured my thoughts into those films especially with regard to our world, society and our nation. I really believe that patriotism is something that we are inborn with. You don't have to tell a child that he is an Indian and he should be proud to be one. What needs to be inculcated in us is nationalism because that is dormant in all of us. This needs to be given more lift and power. We need to make people realise how we need to work for the upliftment (*sic*) of our country. So for me these things are very important and if I can bring those themes in while telling an entertaining story then why not?

Ashutosh Gowariker to Anuradha Sengupta on in.news.yahoo.com, viewed on Feb 26, 2008

Earlier, Gowariker's *Lagaan* (2001) set the human being against the empire. It reinvented the notion of battle by reminding us that sports are subliminal wars. The cricketers or "warriors" stand in various aggressive positions as they stare out from the space of the poster. Aamir Khan, the star and the producer of the film, dominates the poster. He stares out at us, his face sweaty with effort, eyes squinched against the glare of the sun. This is the face of the *karmayogi*, the man who sees action as his religious duty. Nation-building, which is suggested here by the metaphor of welding together a team from a group of disparate players of different caste identities, is thirsty work. The subliminal message is clearer because it is not driven home with a sledgehammer.

While it is easy to dismiss many of these films as jingoistic and shrill, Bollywood can also spring some surprises. Consider how an ordinary romantic film like *Hum Dono* (1961, Amarjeet) that dealt with a case of mistaken identities, included a meditation on war as spoken by Major Verma (Dev Anand) to another captain in the army (played again by Dev Anand):

"Woh kaunsi taaqat hai, Captain, jo hamein apne gharon se, apne pyaar se, apne maa baap se, door door laakar, kandhon pe bandooke rakhne ko majboor kar deti hain? Haalaki hum jaante hain ki jung buri hai, hinsa buri hai, nafrat buri hai, pet ki aag ya shaurat ki bhook ya desh ka pyaar? Ya hamaari insaaniyat, jo haiwaaniyat ke khilaaf bhadak uththi hai? Insaan ke andar ka loha apni chamak dikhaane ke liye mauqe ki taat mein rehta hai aur jab mauqa aata hai to woh yeh nahin dekhta ki uski biwi ka dil tootta hai, ya uski maa ka dil tootta hai ya uski premika ka dil tootta hai ya..."
(What force is this, Captain, that drags us from our homes, our loves, our parents and brings us here and puts guns to our shoulders? When we know that war is wrong, that violence is wrong, that hatred is wrong? Is it hunger or hunger for fame or the love of one's country? Or is it our humanity that revolts against beastliness in others? The streak of iron inside each man waits for the opportunity to show itself. And when that opportunity arises, he does not consider whether his mother's heart will break, or his wife's heart will break or his lover's heart will break or...)

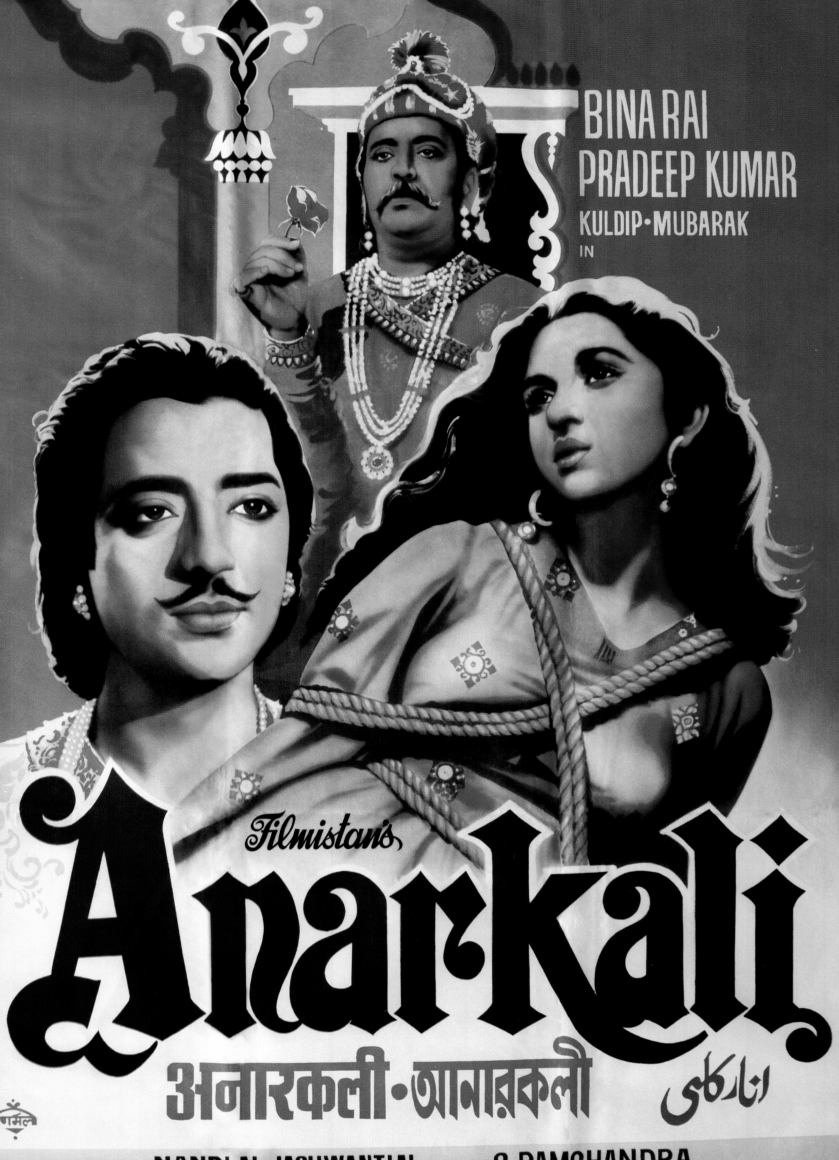

THE WRITER-DIRECTOR OF THE ACADEMY AWARD® NOMINATED 'LAGAAN' AND THE CRITICALLY ACCLAIMED 'SWAD...'

Jodhaa

A
RAJPUT PRINCESS

www.jodhaaakbar.com   IN CINEMAS 25TH JANUARY, 2008

OM THE WRITER-DIRECTOR OF THE ACADEMY AWARD® NOMINATED 'LAGAAN' AND THE CRITICALLY ACCLAIMED 'SWADES'

Akbar

A
MUGHAL EMPEROR

IN CINEMAS 25TH JANUARY, 2008

www.jodhaaakbar.com

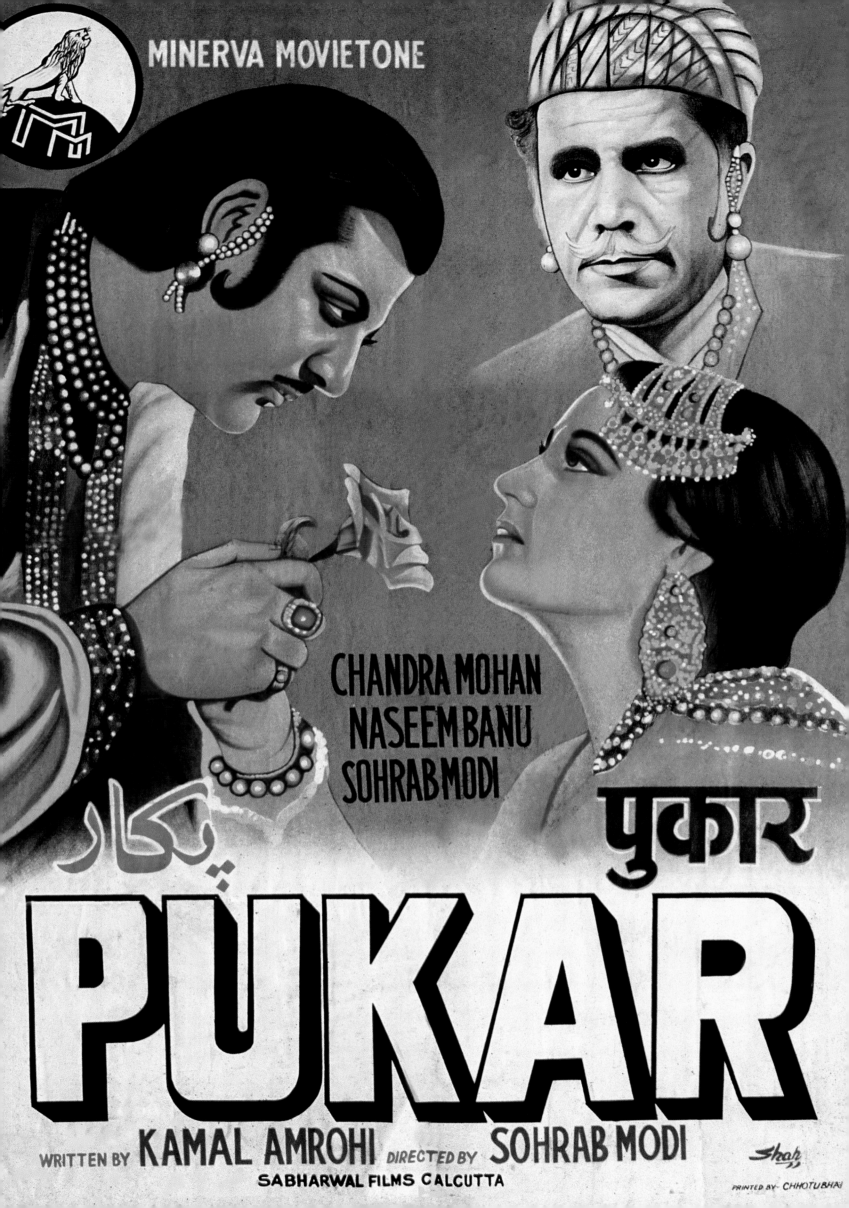

मुग़लेआज़म

STERLING INVESTMENT CORPORATION
PRIVATE LIMITED.,
PRESENTS

K. ASIF'S

MUGHAL-E-AZAM

MUSIC
NAUSHAD

स्टरलिंग इनवेस्टमेंट कारपोरेशन प्राइवट लिमिटेड प्रस्तुत करते है
के.आसिफ कृत
मुग़ले आज़म
مغل اعظم
STERLING INVESTMENT CORPORATION (PVT.) LTD., PRESENTS
K. ASIF's
MUGHAL-E-AZAM

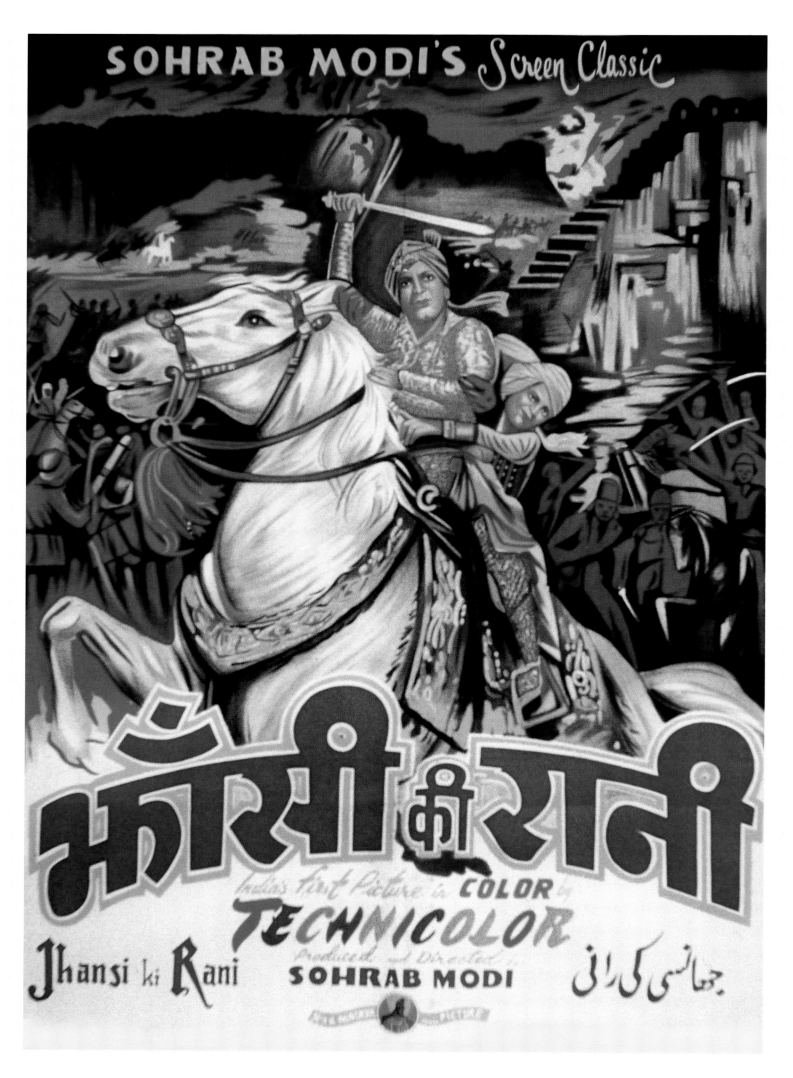

A.K. MISRA PRESENTS
Kamal Amrohi's
रज़िया सुल्तान
Razia Sultan
70 M.M. (EASTMANCOLOR)
STEREOPHONIC SOUND
MUSIC
Khayyam
DIRECTOR OF PHOTOGRAPHY
R.D.mathur
A PICTURE OF
RAJDHANI FILMS (P.) LTD.

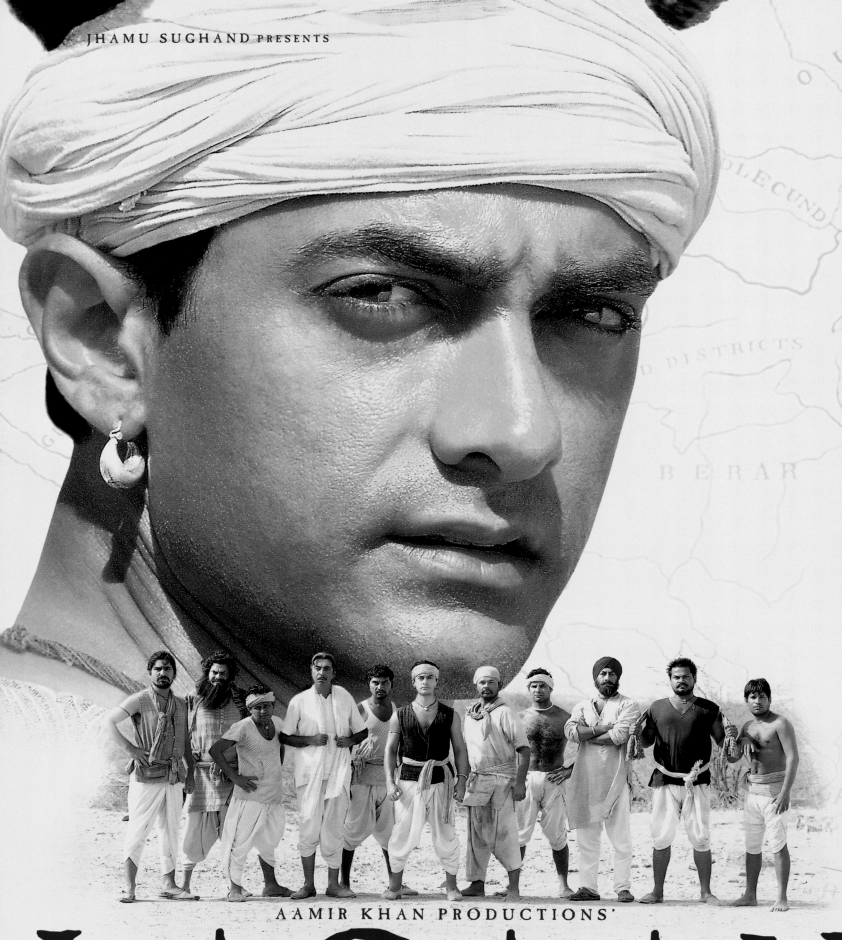

अशोक

FROM THE WRITER & DIRECTOR OF 'LAGAAN'

UTV MOTION PICTURES PRESENTS
ASHUTOSH GOWARIKER PRODUCTIONS'

Swades
We, the people

WRITTEN AND DIRECTED BY ASHUTOSH GOWARIKER

UTV MOTION PICTURES
PRESENTS

RAKEYSH OMPRAKASH MEHRA'S

Rang
De Basanti

India - a generation awakens

Sun Rich Productions
Present
RAJ KITGHLU
DAMAYANTI
PREMIJI & ANSARI
in
एक कदम
EK KADAM

ایک قدم

Direction

RAMNIK DESAI

DIFFERENT STROKES

By common consent, the 1950s represent the golden age of Hindi cinema. Films made then represented the perfect blend between social conscience and commercial sentiment. Filmmakers could explore important films on social issues of the day and still please the men who were backing them.

So Bimal Roy made *Sujata* (1959) about the stranglehold caste had on society, Raj Kapoor examined the plight of the homeless in *Shree 420* (1955), Guru Dutt attacked society's marginalization of the artist and its commodification of love in *Pyaasa* (1957) while creating box-office history. It was an era in which the critical and commercial success of a film seemed linked.

The 1950s were therefore a period of excellence in cinema. Directors did not see glamour and gloss as central to the filmmaking enterprise. They surrounded themselves with writers of a progressive bent and impressive literary talent. But this is true only of great filmmakers, not of those who produced the run-of-the-mill Bollywood film. That product, with its implausible plots, hammy acting, physical humour, arbitrary song sequences and broad, melodramatic brush-strokes would not seem out of place today.

In the 1960s, as the nation-building impulse waned and titans fell by the wayside, a certain lightness of being invaded the cinema. By the next decade, all was surface, all was gloss. Bollywood's reach had become immense. This led, in an almost Hegelian way, to the revolution.

A young advertising filmmaker called Shyam Benegal threw the first stone with *Ankur* (1973), a film that laid bare the neo-feudal relationship of land-owner and labourer. Over the next decade, Benegal was to craft what was then called parallel cinema, a genre looked at with a mixture of contempt and yearning by mainstream masala moviemakers. Benegal's oeuvre stretches from *Manthan* (1976), a film about the formation of milk cooperatives, to *Zubeidaa* (2001), about a Rajasthani royal family and its brush with Bollywood. As an advertising man, the posters crafted for these films were often of a high quality. He inspired a whole generation of filmmakers but these young men and women found very little room for manoeuvre in an industry that was satisfied with the status quo and only interested in returns.

Through the 1980s and 1990s, many talented young directors either gave up the fight or turned to television where they scripted and directed some serials that have become classics of their kind. Many of those who began promisingly turned commercial with a vengeance. Though Mahesh Bhatt's first film *Saaraansh* (1984) took an unsentimental look at the despair of an old couple whose son has died suddenly, he was soon swept into making action flicks and remakes of western crowd-pleasers. Similarly, Govind Nihalani's debut film *Aakrosh* (1980) looked at the criminal justice system and atrocities committed against outcastes, but he was soon making films like *Karma Yudha* (1982). The art-house movement began to fizzle out and was declared dead.

Today, changed equations bring a new set of filmmakers and stories to the fore. A DVD retail revolution has ushered world cinema into India and created a small but powerful audience segment willing to pay well if what it gets is good cinema. Glossy high-octane entertainers still remain big risk-big return ventures, yet there is room for a film like *Hazaaron Khwaishein Aisi* (2003, Sudhir Mishra), set during the storms of then Prime Minister Indira Gandhi's suspension of democracy in the 1970s. Or *Iqbal* (2005, Nagesh Kukunoor), about a deaf young man who wants to play cricket.

A million stories may now contend again.

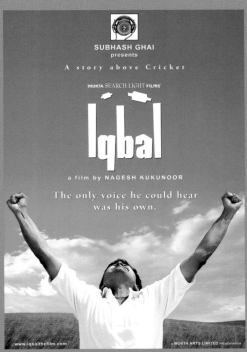

MYTHOLOGY

I t was in my school days that I had seen my first Indian film. It was Dadasaheb Phalke's memorable *Lanka Dahan* tagged to an American feature film at the old West End Cinema of Seth Rustomji Dorabji Wellington situated just behind the Girgaum Police Court. The roadside and the compound of the cinema used to be chockfull with bullock carts in which devoted people from small towns and villages nearby... came to have a darshan of their beloved gods, Shree Ram and Shree Hanuman. As a Westernised Parsi youngster I had a hearty laugh at the sight of a muscular Seeta played by a male artiste (Salunke), as also the all-powerful tail of Shree Hanuman made of rope. But I was stunned by the spectacular burning of Lanka and the thrilling flight of Ram Bhakt in the sky with every shot of the divine flier becoming progressively smaller and smaller to heighten the effect of the sequence.

From JBH Wadia's unpublished biography THOSE WERE THE DAYS

It was at a show of *Life of Christ* that the Indian film industry was born. Dadasaheb ("respected grandfather") Phalke was watching the film and wondering why stories from Hindu mythology could not be similarly told. And so the Indian film industry was created when he made his first feature film, *Raja Harishchandra* (1913). It was based on a story from the great Indian epic, the *Mahabharata,* in which the gods test the fidelity and integrity of a king who passes with such flying colours that he is now a metaphor for uprightness of character and honesty. Phalke advertised it as "A performance with 57,000 photographs. A picture two miles long. All for only three annas."

For a long time, Hindi cinema was dominated by films that dealt with the gods and their doings (the mythologicals) or the saints and devotees of the gods (the devotionals). For our purpose, we have taken the genre to include films about the gods, as well as films about secular saints who might be historical figures such as Sai Baba of Shirdi or Sant Tukaram and so do not belong to the arena of mythology but evoke religious feelings of a similar nature.

This is India, the birthplace of several major world religions, so there is no such thing as a film without some mention of religion, even if it is only implicit in the caste identities suggested by the names of the characters. Further complications arise because the gods often make guest appearances in mainstream Hindi films. One of Amitabh Bachchan's most famous diatribes is addressed to Lord Shiva when he brings the body of his dying mother to the temple in *Deewaar* (1975, Yash Chopra), one of India's best gangster noir films. In a mad romp such as *Amar Akbar Anthony* (1977, Manmohan Desai), the eyes of the statue of the secular saint Shirdi ke Sai Baba emit two flames that literally illuminate the eyes of the blind mother of the three young men of the title. In *Yehi Hai Zindagi* (1977, KS Sethumadhavan), Lord Krishna appears to an atheist and grants him his wish (great wealth); the atheist discovers that with great wealth comes family discord (and health problems, including piles).

The *Ramayana* and the *Mahabharata* represent the fountainheads of Indian storytelling and overwhelmingly influence the audio-visual media. The *Ramayana*'s story of a man who falls in love, enjoys a brief period of exaltation with his beloved, loses her and then must conquer various obstacles in order to win her back, has become the primary story of Bollywood. Looked at another way, the *Ramayana* is equally the story of a hero who fights and conquers the forces of evil. Television also seems to have taken the *Mahabharata* as its model. Most popular soap operas are about a family that is divided and whose members win only Pyrrhic victories against each other.

In the early years of cinema, hundreds of religious films were made. Some of these were of outstanding quality. *Sant Tukaram* (1936, Vishnupant Damle and Sheikh Fatehlal) and *Sant Dnyaneshwar* (1940, Damle and Fatehlal) still stand as brilliant examples of cinematic craft and art. However, after this early high-point was reached, the genre declined in quality. The special effects became shoddy. No attention was paid to period details and the audience simply drifted away. The mythological began to collapse into a formula.

The devotee, or *bhakt*, was always the underdog who suffered the slings and arrows of outrageous fortune but never took up arms against them. Instead, she or he prayed, waited and often sang a number of plaintive songs. In these sufferings, the viewers were supposed to see a reflection of their lives. These devotees would often be represented on the posters in positions suggesting they were performing *puja*, rituals designed to please or appease the gods. Often, direct instructions were given to the faithful as to the nature of the worship required by a deity. For instance, in *Jai Maa Vaishnodevi* (1995, Shantilal Soni), devotees are told quite clearly that failure to worship at the shrine of Bhaironath – the sadhu who pursued Vaishnodevi and tried to persecute her followers – would mean incomplete worship of the goddess.

After the glory years, it was something of a given that these films would attract a largely female audience. This is partly because of the Indian notion that women are naturally more religious and partly because such films were approved viewing by the same patriarchy that controlled the money in most families and so controlled the buying of tickets. However, since going to the movies was also a family experience, and such films would be considered unexceptionable for the young and the old, filmmakers put in a song or two by some divine seductress for the delectation of the men. Thus it was not unusual to find the legendary screen vamp Helen turning up in the films and on the posters, suggesting that pleasures other than the purely spiritual were also on offer. Kobita Sarkar, who wrote a memoir of her years as a censor, *You Can't Please Everyone! Film Censorship: The Inside Story*, discovered that "... all sorts of sexual cavorting was justified if it was cloaked in a 'mythological' garb".

The suffering *bhakt* was very often a woman. This brought about considerable catharsis though the lack of attention to detail. Shoddy special effects and uninspiring music marked them as B-grade films. But they continued to be made in a steady stream, often slightly altering known stories or even creating new ones. This might well be a human need, as Rachel Dwyer points out:

The cinema may not present the orthodox versions of the myths but it presents popularly held beliefs, the episodes people like to turn to for fundamental stories which can be applied to their daily lives, in a manner which is easy to follow as it may be in the style of other popular genres such as television serials. Thus many family problems are likened to the Ramayana, a motif which appears frequently in the social film in an allegorical form, but which is shown directly in the mythological film. These myths answer life's major questions and give us stories to live by as much as stories we spin ourselves through psychoanalysis or whatever other means we choose. One does not have to believe in the stories any more than Freud believed in the Greek myths (Oedipus and others) he used to tell his own stories for our times, or we may not believe in Spiderman though we may believe there is a hero inside us who can fight against injustice.

From FILMING THE GODS: RELIGION AND INDIAN CINEMA by Rachel Dwyer

This is a timely warning against those who would take acts of piety as the behaviour of "simple people" acting out "simple faith". For Hinduism is not a simple faith. Nor is Islam but there have been few, if any, films that deal directly with Islam because of the prohibition against showing or depicting the Prophet. (Islamicate films, as they are now called, will be discussed in some detail in the chapter on fantasy.)

The posters of these films were therefore almost directly inspired by the Raja Ravi Varma School of art with its many imitators in the lithograph makers across the country. No attempt was made to represent the actors who played gods and goddesses in the film. The standardized North Indian face that the nobleman from Kerala created, sufficed for film after film, for everyone from Durga to Vaishnodevi Maa.

The poster makers might well argue that traditional iconography also works on the same principles. We tell the gods apart from what they wear or carry or by what they are represented. Thus we know Lord Brahma by his beard or Lord Shiva by the snake around his neck, just as the devoted Roman Catholic might recognize St Catherine by her wheel or St Sebastian by the arrows protruding from his body. Poster artists also did not hesitate to incorporate sacred symbols and designs, such as the six-petalled lotus in *Mahapavan Teerth Yatra* (1975, Vijay Sharma), with deities in the petals to suggest that such a pilgrimage (*teerth yatra*) would invoke the blessings of these gods.

When *Jai Santoshi Maa* (1975, Vijay Sharma) exploded on screens all over the country, the hysteria it generated was different from anything that had ever preceded it. Women formed clubs and creches so that they could watch the film at leisure and not have to depend on their husbands to take them to see it. There were some cinemas in which a film had never celebrated a jubilee run but in which *Jai Santoshi Maa* astonishingly managed to run for 50 weeks. There was nothing to explain how this film became such a phenomenon. It was made on a shoestring budget with obvious studio sets and special effects that did not quite match the standards set by Damle and Fatehlal who worked nearly 30 years earlier. It did not have the exploitative sequences of other films; all the songs were devotional in intent. One of these, "*Main toh aarti utaaroon re, Santoshi Maa ki*" (I will perform a ritual of worship in honour of Mother Santoshi), has now actually become anthemic. Other gods and goddesses have also had their praises sung in the same tune with words that are tweaked in order to suit the new deity.

The story of *Jai Santoshi Maa* was not original either. According to it, Santoshi Devi is created when the sons of Lord Ganesha find themselves without a sister to tie *rakhis* on their wrists. (The *rakhi* is a band of protection, a symbolic promise of protection given by a brother to his sister.) She enjoys the combined powers of Mahalaxmi, Saraswati and Parvati, and becomes a very powerful goddess who attracts a growing number of devotees. Finally, Narad Muni, the messenger of the gods known to eternally cause trouble, warns the three that the people's devotion to the new goddess is so strong that they are now out of the pale. He tells them that the most faithful of Santoshi Maa's worshippers is Satyavati and they decide to test her through a series of ordeals. She emerges with her faith unaffected and the trio reveal their true intent: they only wished to test Satyavati's faith so that she might emerge as a paragon of virtue; they were not really jealous of Santoshi Devi.

Shirdi Ke Sai Baba (1977, Ashok Bhushan), which followed the life of the enigmatic and secular saint from Maharashtra, Sai Baba, was another blockbuster. The story begins with a young couple whose child is dying. The child recovers for a brief period and asks to be taken to Shirdi. On the way, they are told the story of Sai Baba, a saint reciting scriptures from several different traditions, who invoked the blessings of Allah on his Hindu devotees and those of Krishna on his Muslim followers.

Hundreds of unsuccessful attempts were made to re-create the success of *Jai Santoshi Maa and Shirdi Ke Sai Baba*, including remakes of both these films in the 2000s. (The new films retained both the names and the general spirit of the older ones.) But with the phenomenal success of Ramanand Sagar's television serialization of the *Ramayana* and BR Chopra's *Mahabharata*, it seems as if the gods have now found a home on Indian television.

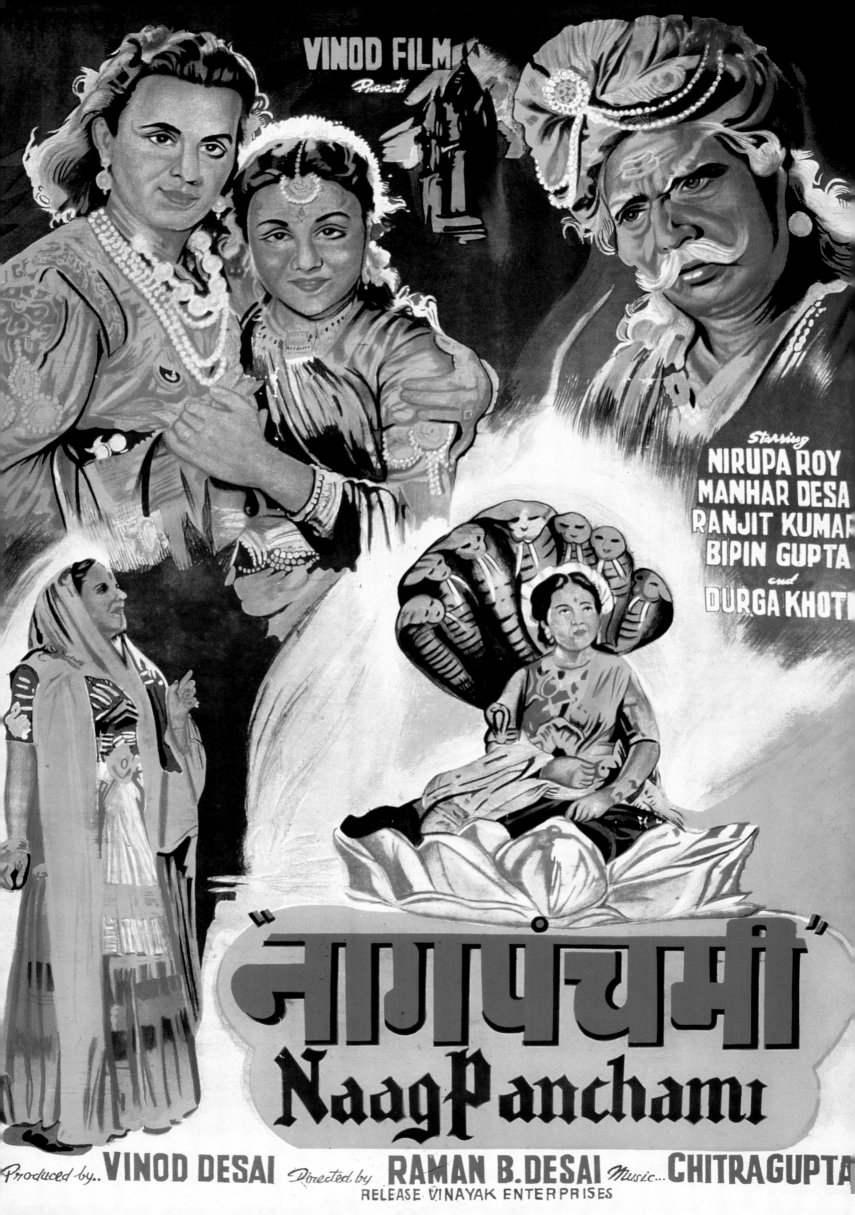

Snake Charmers

In Hindu mythology, the serpent does not have as bad a reputation as it does in the Judaeo-Christian tradition. It is a snake on which Lord Vishnu, one of the divine triumvirate, rests. It is a snake that is wound around the neck of Lord Shiva. It is a snake that offers to be the rope that turns Mount Meru when the sea has to be churned to yield the nectar of immortality sought by gods and demons alike.

In Buddhist belief, the Nagas were protective deities. In many of these cases, the snake represented in popular art forms is the cobra or the king cobra.

Thus the snake is not a metaphor but an actual animal presence. The only exception to this rule is *Zehreela Insaan* (1974, SR Puttana Kanagal), which is a romance with no mythological connotations at all. Here it is the hero who is the rebel figure, a bruised and therefore bruising young man, who is seen as poisonous. The use of the snake's scales on the poster (*page 161*) represents something of a first, since it is generally the form rather than the pattern of the snakeskin that is used.

There are two kinds of mythological snakes that have cast their spell over Bollywood. In the first instance, the snake is associated with Lord Shiva. *Karwa Chauth* (1980, Ramlal Hans), for instance, has the heroine giving birth to a healthy baby. Her scheming sisters-in-law replace the child with a snake. Though she sees what she has wrought, she puts the snake to her breast. Pleased with such devotion, Lord Shiva blesses her. Her husband, who has been missing in action, is returned to her as well. There is a clear association between the godhead and the cobra hood. Here, the snake is masculine, like his brothers in western mythology.

But the other snake has a clearly feminine presence. This is the *ichchadaari* snake which can change shape at will because, according to myth, she or he has spent two or three hundred years in prayer and meditation.

The best example of the snake film is *Nagin* (1976, Raj Kumar Kohli). Professor Vijay (Sunil Dutt) shoots a hawk that is attacking a snake. The snake turns into a human being (Jeetendra) who rewards Vijay by inviting him to the mating dance of the *ichchadaari* snakes, which is to take place that night. Instead of going alone as he has promised, Vijay brings along several male friends and they watch as the two snakes in human form writhe about in the moonlight. But when the male turns back into his snake form, one of the young men shoots him in a chivalrous attempt to save the woman who has not changed back yet. This sends the female snake (Reena Roy) off on a mission of vengeance as she has seen in her dying lover's eyes images of the men who killed him. The snake is at the centre of the poster's pictorial space, but the stars animate the image.

Posters for this kind of film always have a woman with her arms raised above her head, hands cupped to mimic the hood of a cobra. This is to indicate that she is now performing the snake dance, spoofed with great brilliance in *Monsoon Wedding* (2001, Mira Nair).

As might be expected from a largely patriarchal cinema, it is a man who tames this snake, usually with a *been* (the wind instrument snake charmers play in India). She hears the insistent whine of the *been*, generally in a song, and is drawn by its sound. It is often the only way to uncover an *ichchadaari naagin*. The movie *Nagin* suggests looking at her in a mirror where she can be seen as a snake, rather than the comely human form she has chosen to adopt.

Snake films moult at regular intervals but they never die. They cast off their old skins and emerge, rejuvenated by a heroine with suitably large eyes, an ability to dance well, a good music score and a male desire to deploy feminine rage in a new cinematic form.

ROMANCE

I t has often been said that the majority of Hindi films are about love. That makes Bollywood no different from cinema in most parts of the world. Love, whether requited or not, consummated or not, legendary or contemporary, is the driving force behind thousands of celluloid narratives. In India, this preoccupation with love has often given rise to talk of the formula. Those who do not understand the rhythms of Indian storytelling summarize it thus: a young man and a young woman fall in love. Circumstances, largely in the form of their disparate social positions, keep them apart. Once these have been overcome, they marry. In the case of the romantic tragedy, love fails to break the barriers of society and one or both the young people die. This summary ignores the fact that most love stories follow a pattern. The Arabian story of Laila and Majnu holds endless fascination for Indian filmmakers. The *Laila Majnu* poster is the latest in a long line of retellings of the tale of the lover who grew mad and wandered into the desert to die. *Laila Majnu* was made twice as a silent film in India, in 1922 and 1927. It was made four times in Hindi, in 1931, in 1945, then in 1953 and finally in 1976 (the one featured here).

The classic Bollywood plotline follows a well-worn path, which allows viewers to sit back and enjoy the journey and the variations on the old theme. For instance, each hero will believe himself to be unloved. Each will sing a sad song. Together these songs of grief and heartbreak have formed a coherent and beautiful oeuvre of music that animates much of North India in a lasting genre of popular culture.

In many ways, this "formula" represents a society struggling with several conflicts. On one side is the family with its wide network of business associations and ability to provide for all; on the other is love, which speaks to the individual and prioritizes the self. The loved object is set on a pedestal and both the worshipper and the worshipped are transcendent. The ordinary rules of society do not apply, so the family was only a hindrance. Love therefore represented much more than an amorous liaison between two healthy young animals. It represented the tensions of the State, the siren call of the Self, although the land of the lotus-eaters for the upper classes was the family. To fall in love was to ignore the call of duty. It was to reverse the hierarchy of precedence in which the nation came first, the clan next, the family thereafter and the self last.

Beyond this, the way the love story was framed had much to say about how Indian society saw wealth. The rich young man in many Hindi films is surrounded by wealth but he is always emotionally impoverished. His family is also represented as evil; they only want his wealth. Whether it was *Prince* (1969, Lekh Tandon), *Bobby* (1973, Raj Kapoor) or *Jab We Met* (2007, Imtiaz Ali), the rich young man is to be pitied for his sterile world. This also helped console the middle-class in its daily privations. While in earlier decades the hero would find love in the arms of a poor girl, *Jab We Met* redefines notions of wealth and poverty. The hierarchy is maintained, for the heroine is from a farming family. She comes from bourgeois comfort but he is heir to a substantial fortune. The difference is between their access to self-esteem, their ability to enjoy the world. Her loving family empowers her; his devastated family suffocates him. The message: wealth is no longer bad and the wealthy are just like us, only richer.

In many films the conflict between love and the family is sorted out by a little trickery. The hero or heroine runs away from an arranged marriage. On the way, he or she encounters a good-looking young stranger of the opposite sex. They fall in love and in the end the runaway discovers that the good-looking stranger was the person chosen by his or her parents. This helps maintain the status quo – your parents know what is good for you – while allowing for a picaresque journey to love. Love was recognized as anarchic but it was also represented as something "natural". Many posters for romantic films have elements of nature to emphasize this connection. The *Aradhana* (1969, Shakti Samanta) poster makes the relationship between love and nature clearer. There are flowers in the poster, that form a garland, but not quite. The garland is symbolic of marriage. In *Parineeta* (made in 1953 and 2005, by Bimal Roy and Pradeep Sarkar respectively), the heroine's playful act of throwing some flowers strung together around the neck of the young man with whom she has grown up, leads her to believe she is married to him. The somewhat dissolute aspect of these flowers may be seen as a reflection of the then daring nature of the theme of *Aradhana*; the film itself dealt with the consequences of sex before marriage.

In the 1950s, love was a spiritual thing. Amorous glances might be explained but love was chivalric, melancholic, idealized; it was more agony than ecstasy. Some observers have suggested that this was a result of the intellectual stranglehold that the Left had on cinema at the time. This gave rise to some powerful films indicting society; but the moralizing extended to the sphere of the body as well. By the 1960s the solemnity of the women in white, the aphysical wraiths who flitted across our screens as symbols of inviolable purity, gave way to a more playful woman. The films themselves went through an adolescent phase where the relationship between men and women became teasing. Posters reflected this change in the way the stars were now dressed. They no longer wore Indian clothes, which until then, had been clear markers of status and caste positions. Here, the clothes spoke of a westernized class of people. This playfulness also allowed for more spaces for passion and for the "natural" untamed self.

In the 1970s the romantic film took a beating at the hands of action cinema in which the female leads were plot ornaments only. Romance would be revived by occasional films such as *Bobby* or *Julie* (1975, KS Sethumadhavan), both of which had on-screen Christian heroines. Since Christians are held to be westernized (read, alienated

from Indian values, and therefore immoral), Dimple Kapadia as Bobby and Lakshmi as Julie were dressed in mini skirts and other revealing clothes. Both were made to enact scenes few established heroines would have agreed to. Bobby is kissed on the mouth, always a problematic moment in the career of a Hindi film heroine; Julie gets pregnant after some steamy rolling about in a bed. However, the leitmotif of the 1970s was violence. It was only after a 20-year blood fest that romance returned in the early 1990s. The uber male of these decades began to be replaced by a likeable young man, often played by Saif Ali Khan in films like *Salaam Namaste* (2005, Siddharth Anand) and *Hum Tum* (2004, Kunal Kohli). Where once he surveyed his woman with a possessive air, the hero now looks bemused when confronted by the heroine. A new gender agenda is being played out.

Or is it? Central to the romantic enterprise was the figure of the woman, the female protagonist or the heroine. Through the course of this essay she has been referred to as the heroine, as she is often that: the figure carrying the burden of the story, for whom audience identification is sought and whose trials and tribulations form the centre of the story. In poster after poster, it becomes apparent that she would take over the space of the story. Even the hero's sufferings, if any, would be related directly to her. There were some films in which the male lead, as we will call him out of a sense of courtesy, did seem to play as important a role. In *Barsaat*, the female form (Nargis) is bent over the arm of the hero (Raj Kapoor) in surrender, but the whole construct became the logo of the RK Studio.

This positioning was also visible in the way posters were structured. In *Chandni* (1989, Yash Chopra), Sridevi takes up all the poster space, stretching her arms out in an *angdaai*, a sensuous stretch enshrined in *prakrit* or folk poetry and Hindi film lyrics. The male leads feature nowhere. Generally, this happens when the star is at her zenith; which was not the case here. Sridevi had not had a successful release for two years before *Chandni*. She seems to be emerging from a rose, the eternal symbol of love. It is a pink rose, not a red one, and though this decision was probably not semiotic, it points again to innocence. In many Indian traditions, pink is the colour of spring. This in turn serves as a metaphor for a young woman's readiness for love.

The re-release poster for *Pakeezah* shows the white of Meena Kumari's clothes spilling into the rest of the frame. If you consider that *pakeezah* means "the pure one", it seems apposite even if Kamal Amrohi did not mean the name to refer to his heroine. The pure one was the little girl who watches the wedding procession that has come to take Sahibjan (Meena Kumari) from the *kotha* (the house of dance). These posters give the lie to one of the greatest myths of a patriarchal studio system: that a woman could not sell a film. In most of them, the woman is given more space than the man. The burden of the romantic film's success was placed on her shoulders. She bore it well.

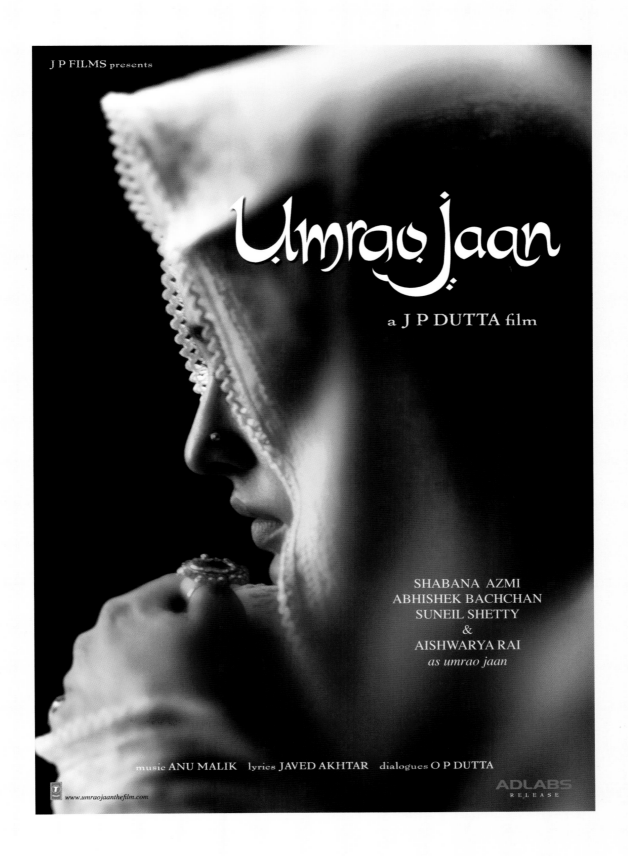

GURU DUTT FILMS LIMITED
PRESENTS

MALA SINHA · GURU DUTT
JOHNNY WALKER · WAHEEDA REHMAN

Pyaasa

MUSIC BY S. D. BURMAN LYRICS BY SAHIR
DIRECTION
GURU DUTT

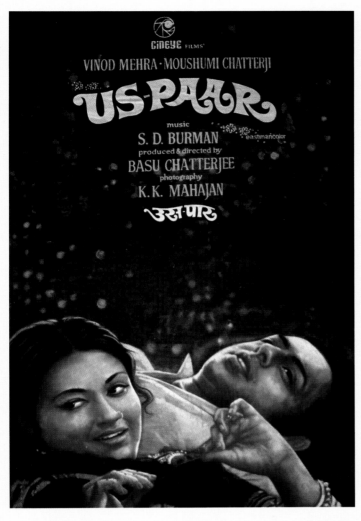

CINEYE FILMS'
VINOD MEHRA · MOUSHUMI CHATTERJI
US PAAR
music
S. D. BURMAN
eastmancolor
produced & directed by
BASU CHATTERJEE
photography
K. K. MAHAJAN
उस पार

DEVANAND · NUTAN IN
Nav Ketan's
TERE GHAR KE SAMNE
WRITTEN & DIRECTED BY VIJAY ANAND
तेरे घर के सामने MUSIC S.D.BURMAN LYRICS HASRAT

के. पी. के. मूवीज़ कृत
परिवार
ईस्टमनकलर में
निर्माता और दिग्दर्शक
केवल पी. कश्यप
संगीत
कल्याणजी आनन्दजी
पटकथा-संवाद
ब्रिज कत्याल
गीत
गुलशन बावरा

विजय आनन्द कृत
तेरे मेरे सपने
संगीत
एस. डि. बर्मन
कैमरा
वी. रात्रा
नवकेतन इन्टरप्राईजेज़ का चित्र

FILMISTAN LTD.

NALINI JAYWANT
DEV ANAND
NIRUPA ROY AND PRAN
in

MUNIM JI
मुनीमजी

LYRICS SAHIR LUDHIANVI SHAILENDRA
MUSIC S. D. BURMAN

Directed by SUBODH MUKERJI

शर्मिला टैगोर • राजेश खन्ना • सुजीत कुमार और फरीदा जलाल

शक्ति फिल्म्स का

आराधना

ईस्टमनकलर में

निर्माता एवं निर्देशक
शक्ति सामन्ता
संगीत
एस. डी. बर्मन

Amar Chhaya PRESENTS RAJESH KHANNA · RAAKHEE IN

शहजादा
SHEHZADA
EASTMANCOLOR

DIRECTED BY   MUSIC   DIALOGUES-LYRICS   PRODUCED BY
K. SHANKAR   R. D. BURMAN   RAJINDER KRISHAN   SURINDER KAPOOR

धर्मेन्द्र • हेमा मालिनी

SA सेवन आर्ट्स पिक्चर्स कृत

राजा जानी
ईस्टमनकलर में

निर्माता
मोहन सहगल
संगीत
लक्ष्मीकांत प्यारेलाल
गीत
मदन मोहला

RAJA
JANI

MALA SINHA
RAAJ KUMAR
JEETENDRA
JOHNNY WALKER
Movie Mughals'
Mere Huzoor
eastmancolor
मेरे हुज़ूर
میرے حضور
STORY, SCREENPLAY DIALOGUE, DIRECTION
VINOD KUMAR
MUSIC
SHANKER · JAIKISHAN
PRODUCED BY
MALIK CHAND KOCHAR & VINOD KUMAR

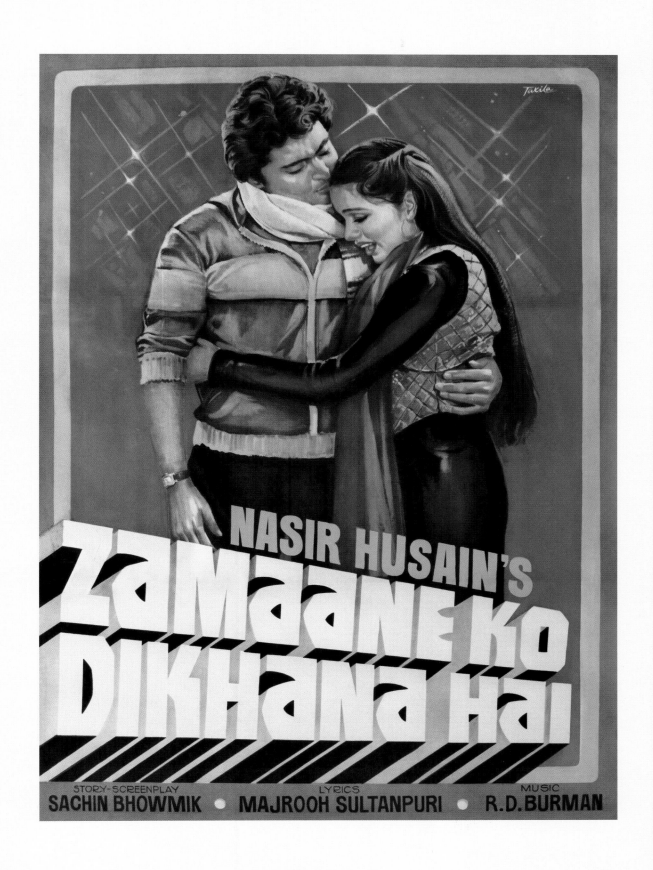

SHAMMI KAPOOR SHARMILA TAGORE & PRAN IN

Shakti FILMS PRESENT

an EVENING in PARIS

EASTMANCOLOR

PRODUCED - DIRECTED BY
SHAKTI SAMANTA
MUSIC
SHANKER JAIKISHAN

पॅरिस की एक शाम

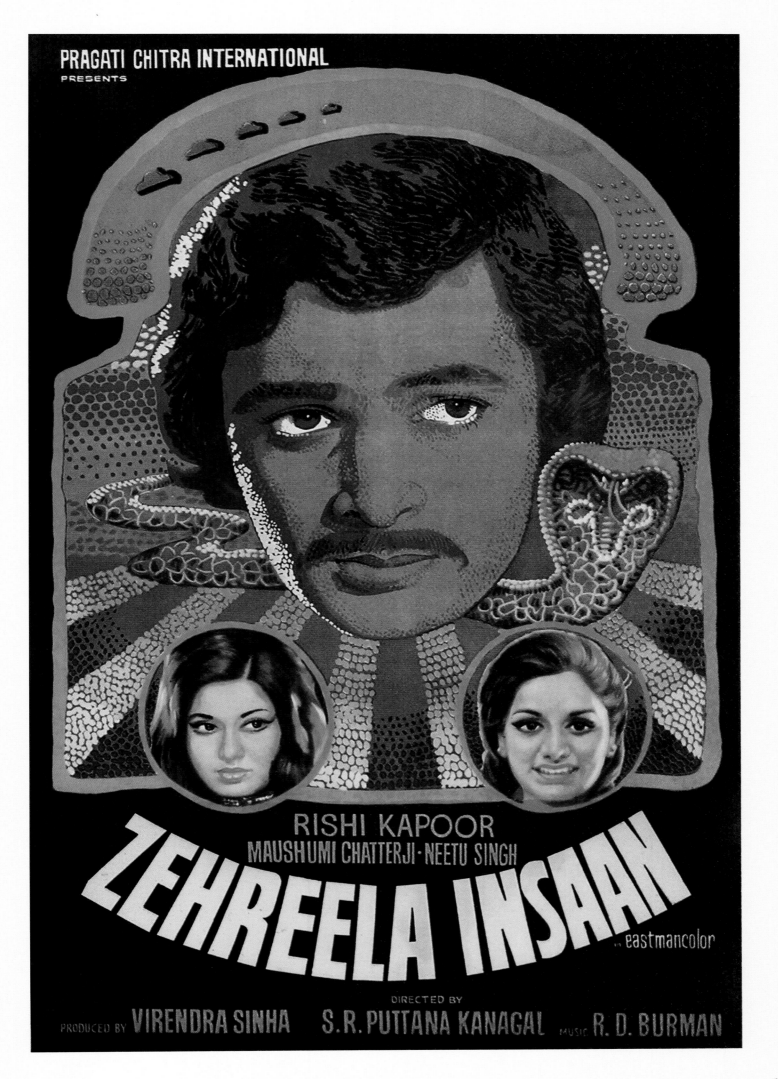

PRAGATI CHITRA INTERNATIONAL
PRESENTS

RISHI KAPOOR
MAUSHUMI CHATTERJI · NEETU SINGH

ZEHREELA INSAAN
in eastmancolor

DIRECTED BY
PRODUCED BY VIRENDRA SINHA   S.R. PUTTANA KANAGAL   MUSIC R.D. BURMAN

DHARMA PRODUCTIONS PRESENTS

KAL HO NAA HO

PRODUCED BY **YASH JOHAR**
DIRECTED BY **NIKHIL ADVANI**
MUSIC BY **SHANKAR EHSAAN LOY**
LYRICS BY **JAVED AKHTAR**

CASSETTES AND CDs Sony Music
www.khnhthefilm.com ▪ www.sonymusic.com

Red Chillies Entertainment
presents
a Farah Khan film

OM SHANTI OM

a Farah Khan film

Music Vishal & Shekhar   Lyrics Javed Akhtar   DOP V. Manikandan
Art Sabu Cyril   Sound Nakul Kamte   Editor Shirish Kunder   FP Sanjiv Chawla   Producer Gauri Khan

RAJ KAPOOR
NARGIS

RAJ KAPOOR'S

BARSAAT

बरसात

DIRECTED BY

RAJ KAPOOR

MUSIC

SHANKER-JAI KISHAN

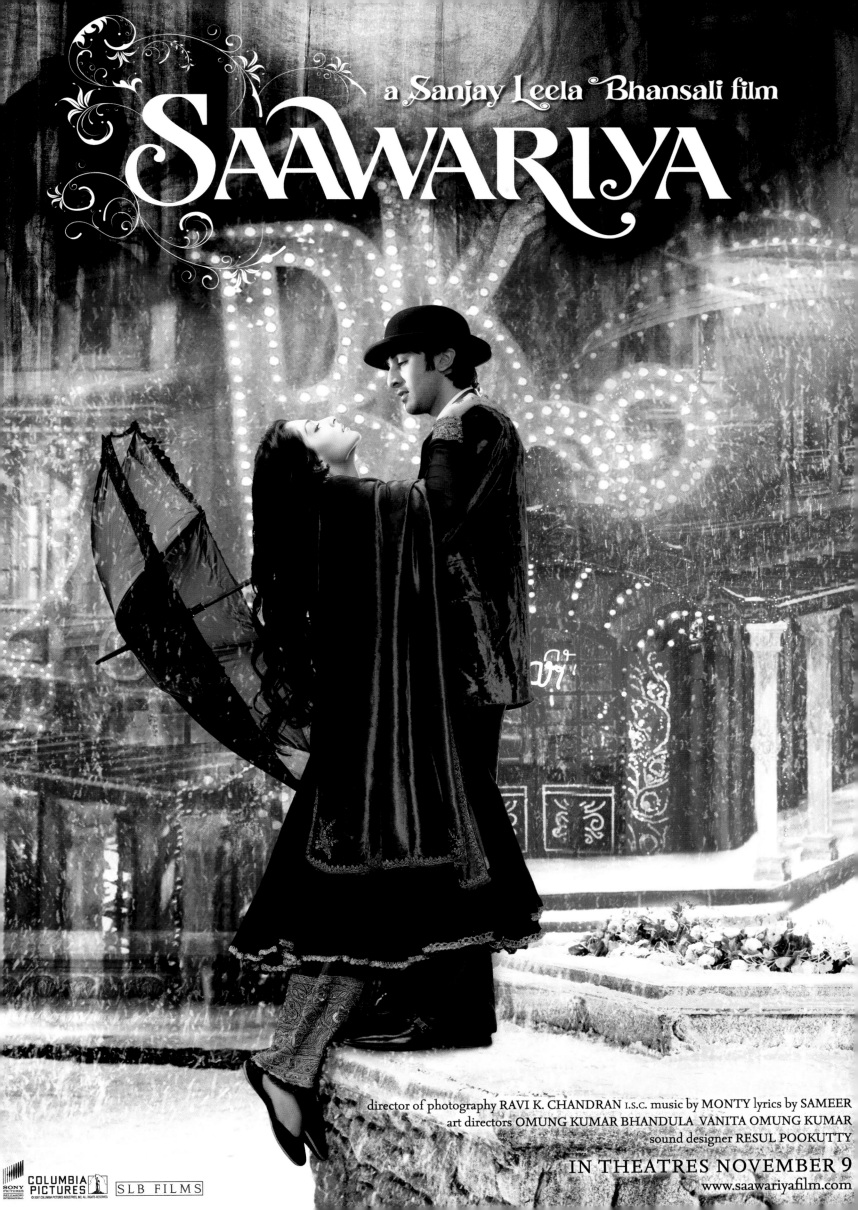

HTA HAI

AN
EXCEL
ENTERTAINMENT
PRODUCTION

MUSIC SHANKAR
EHSAAN LOY

LYRICS
JAVED AKHTAR

DIRECTOR OF PHOTOGRAPHY
RAVI K. CHANDRAN

CO-PRODUCER
PRAVIN TALREJA

PRODUCED BY
RITESH SIDHWANI

STORY, SCREENPLAY, DIALOGUE
& DIRECTION
FARHAN AKHTAR

Bawdy Beautiful

In the beginning was the camera and it was an eye, and the eye was trained on the female body. The camera codified the male gaze, turning flesh into celluloid.

What the cameras began, the posters continued, locating erotic zones and playing them up, often by realigning spatial reality. The woman's body is twisted, bent, reorganized and reshaped so that her breasts and buttocks attract the eye. Often, as in the poster for *Kab? Kyoon? Aur Kahan?* (1970, Arjun Hingorani), the feminine body is dissected and offered as less than the sum of her parts. The idea for this poster, a woman's legs as a frame for the male figure/s in the frame, is a tried and tested one. It had achieved a *succès de scandale* earlier that year for the "progressive" film *Chetana* (1970, B Aar Ishara) and since then the arch created by a woman's legs has stood for an entire range of misogynistic ideas: woman as honey trap, woman as the path to perdition, woman as a sexually controlling monster.

In general, the depiction of the male physique was, for the early decades of cinema, limited to the B-grade movies. It was only in the stunt films or the action films that a man's body mattered. In most other films, only his face represented him. You can see this in the poster for *Chhailla Babu* (1977, Joy Mukherji) where the male star Rajesh Khanna's face takes up as much space as the whole of the female star's body. Zeenat Aman is presented in a position of alluring invitation. The hero's physical self was rarely a matter of much concern. It was enough that he was a man. Thus portly middle-aged men often played college students for decades without causing much cognitive dissonance in the audience. This trend is much more marked in South Indian films.

In many posters that use this appeal to the base instincts, we find the upper bodies of the lead pair presented in tight close-up. This has two functions. It enhances the heroine's attractions, often to the point of physical improbabilitiy. It also plays on the voyeuristic tendency since it brings us into intimate contact with the love scene being played out. Thus such posters were produced mainly for the B-grade films. If the successful heroines of mainstream cinema were to attempt something like this, they would not be happy to see themselves thus depicted on posters. They would throw their sometimes not-inconsiderable star power at the producer to make sure a more sanitized image was made available.

All this changed with the coming of a physicality borrowed from the West. When Zeenat Aman (who stars in two of the posters on the opposite page) arrived in Hindi cinema, she brought with her a new look: the long-legged and slimmer-hipped look of models in the 1970s. By the 1980s, the press had reached the depths of lookism: Sridevi, for instance, was called Miss Thunder Thighs with impunity because she was supposed to be heavier than usual.

Sunny Deol, among the men, was the first to sport a bare chest. Plots were even devised to get him into the swimming pool. He was followed in quick succession by such pectorally perky stars as Salman Khan, Hrithik Roshan and Akshay Kumar. The V-shape, an enhanced torso tapering down to a narrow waist, became the sine qua non of male stardom. The standard female body went through a corresponding change too. Where Leela Naidu remembers that she was sent a rubber bra with two nozzles attached so that they could be blown up to the "required" size, the new look is sleek and svelte. This fits in with the hunger of the new breed: the desire to fit in with the model of Hollywood.

With starlets willing to discuss their plastic surgery openly, a new relationship to the body is being forged. This will no doubt show up in posters as the Photoshop toolkit begins to work its magic.

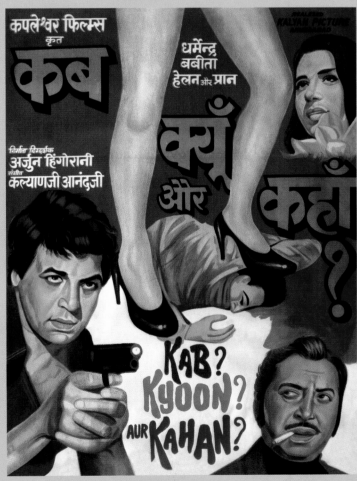

FANTASY

At some level, all cinema is fantasy. One of the great narratives of cinema is the collapse of the rational mind in the darkness of the cinema hall, as we allow ourselves to see the world through the eyes of the director. In so doing, we yield to the fantasy that the images captured by the camera represent a living reality. We respond emotionally and empathically, even as we marvel at the excellence of the special effects or decry the camerawork. This means that we never fully succumb to the illusion and yet are pulled back to it again and again.

Fantasy films in Bollywood tend to draw upon Arabian sources for their plots. The *Thousand and One Nights* has always been a rich mother lode of stories and Bollywood filmmakers have mined it liberally. This should not be surprising since the tales that Scheherezade wove for Prince Shahryar to prevent him from cutting off her head were themselves drawn from diverse sources, including the much older Indian *Jataka Tales*, moral stories that represent the compassionate Buddha's reincarnations in several births and forms to teach humanity a variety of lessons.

Many fantasy films fell into the B-grade category. They were made on shoestring budgets with no stars and poor special effects. In *Aaya Toofan* (1964, Mohammad Hussain), for instance, a globe of extraterrestrial origin appears in the sky. It slowly descends and splits open to reveal a magician within, but not before we have seen the string holding it up for the camera. Nor was anyone terribly careful about the time frame of the film. Even in *Dharam Veer* (1977, Manmohan Desai), Dharam (Dharmendra) wears a Roman subligaculum, the shift with a skirt Roman gladiators wore, while the other hero, Veer (Jeetendra), wears a cavalier shirt and tight-fitting breeches. They fight with rapiers, more a gentleman's duelling device than a soldier's weapon. Despite it being so high-profile a film – it had four major stars and the look of a big-budget movie – there is a sequence in which Dharam abducts the princess Pallavi (Zeenat Aman) on his horse and races to the battlements. Surrounded by her guards, he pushes his mount to leap off the walls and the horse jumps in three separate frames. Although the critics savaged these films, they continued to be made. This meant that they had an audience, even if not an elite one.

The attraction for the filmmakers was clear. They could rewrite the rules in the genre of fantasy. The heroine in Hindi cinema, for instance, had a fixed set of locations in which she was to be found. She could either be in her father's home or in her husband's home. If she was out in the open, it was in the company of her friends, all of them on bicycles, all singing a song which would have to do with the joy of being outdoors. This was muscular Hinduism, adapted from the Boy Scouts and Girl Guides movement. If the heroine appeared anywhere else – a nightclub, a stage – an elaborate rationale had to be presented to justify her being there. (On stage? She was dancing for charity. In a nightclub? She was running for her life.)

In a fantasy film, the princess often simply sneaked out of the palace and mingled with the mob. This yearning for the demotic also consoled the men in the cheap seats. Life in the palaces of the world was such a sterile experience that young women had to seek out the marketplace to find excitement, adventure and the right measure of testosterone. In *Dharam Veer*, for instance, Dharam smears his blood on Pallavi's forehead. She finds it very hard to wipe away for it is the hot and vital blood that flows through peasants and soldiers. Later at the palace, she makes her royal suitor Satpal Singh, played by the veteran villain Jeevan, cut his thumb and smear his forehead with the blood. This is a watery effluvium, wiped away easily. The princess sneers, as well she might. One of the lasting elements of this kind of fantasy is the virility of the farmer and the worker.

The posters for all these films emphasized the otherness of the women in the films. They were shown with wings, as in the poster for *Ek Armaan Mera* (1959, Gunjal). Angels are common in Indian mythology and folktales but are rarely depicted with wings. These are obviously taken from a tradition that finds its home somewhere in the monotheistic religious traditions of the Fertile Crescent. Zoroastrianism, Judaism and Christianity all have angels and Islam finds room for the *farishta* (a figure close to the angel) as well. Where depictions were allowed, the winged angels from our posters would have been familiar. Alladin, Sindbad and Ali Baba were all-time favourites. At some point, they have all been in films, though it took the questionable genius of PN Arora to combine the three in *Sindbad, Alibaba and Aladin* (1965). Hatim Tai, another favourite, was a figure who lived in the time of the prophet Muhammad but did not meet him. Hatim Tai stories generally have to do with the king solving seven riddles that are put to him, a familiar trope in folklore such as the *Vikram Betaal* tales in which a vampire tests King Vikramaditya.

The other powerful influence on the fantasy films of Bollywood came from a most unlikely source. In 1919, Johnston McCulley created Zorro as a character in a novel that was serialized in a pulp weekly. Don Diego Vega, as he was originally called, was the son of a California landlord who fought crime under the name Zorro. Effete by day and dashing by night, Zorro himself owed much to Baroness Orczy's *The Scarlet Pimpernel*. The Hollywood history of Zorro dates back to 1920; in India, the masked figure with the rapier and cloak would find his way into many films. *Awaara Abdulla* (1963, Tara Harish) tells the story of Shera (Dara Singh) who is a prince in exile. When he learns he has the right to the throne, he dresses up like Zorro and heads into town to wrestle with John de Silva (Wrestling Champion of Europe) and Ad Rod Goa (Wrestling Champion of the West Indies). It is evident from the poster of *Toofan* (1975, Kedar Kapoor) that Zorro was a major influence in the shaping of the character played by Vikram. Later, Navin Nischol would reprise the same role and now, with the character out of copyright, the film could even bear the title *Zorro* (1975, Shibu Mitra).

It is easy to see the appeal of Zorro. Here is a character of the upper classes who fights for the poor and downtrodden. In *Toofan*, for instance, Baadal is a happy-go-lucky youth by day but by night he turns into the masked Toofan or "storm", the literal meaning of his name, a nice metaphoric extension of his civilian name, Baadal or "cloud". In another *Toofan* (1989, Ketan Desai), it was Amitabh Bachchan who played the avenger. The cape and mask were a natural extension of the persona that he had carved out over the years. It might be said that the earlier Toofans might have prepared the way for Bachchan's Angry Young Man persona. However, from his first successful film, *Zanjeer*, it became apparent that he was extraordinary in his ability to beat up several men single-handed while still managing to give these incredible feats some measure of credibility. In *Shahenshah* (1988, Tinnu Anand), the disguise was decidedly odd. It consisted of an aged persona, a lock of grey hair and a metal glove. The mundane alter ego was an effete and corrupt police officer.

This trope, of a young man with a double identity, who fights to reorganize the social order, became very popular through the 1980s and 1990s. Even if he were to acquire superpowers, these would be harnessed for the doing of good. Thus in *Mr India* (1987, Shekhar Kapur), the hero Arun (Anil Kapoor) has spent his life running an orphanage in his home. When the deliciously evil Mogambo (Amrish Puri) wants to use the house as storage space for weapons – they never put enough closets into gangster dens, it would seem – he acquires a device from a friend of his father that turns him invisible and allows him to give as good as he gets. As in most of the Zorro films, the heroine (Sridevi) is attracted to Mr India the crime fighter but not to Arun's more quotidian self. Invisible men had appeared in Bollywood before; Kishore Kumar played one in *Mr X in Bombay* (1964, Shantilal Soni) but he had exploited this transparency for its humorous potential rather than its dramatic possibilities.

Science fiction never achieved much success in Bollywood. Perhaps this was because the necessary pre-requisites were not in place. India has seldom been suspicious of the gifts of science as the West has become. Both *Rocket Tarzan* (1963, BJ Patel) and *Kaala Jaadu* (1963, Mahmood) were made as B-grade films. No star would agree to act in them and their special effects would inevitably be so tacky as to be laughable even in their own time. However, their posters have now achieved an almost surreal stylishness that comes from our longing for a bygone age.

In all posters featuring the masked man, the hero is shown with the mask on, thus maintaining the mystery about his identity, although the audience knows that the hero will be the masked man. And since his name will blaze above the titles, the mask is transparent to us. This is part of the illusion of the illusory; and audiences play along, willing to enjoy the swashbuckling in Cloud Cuckoo Land.

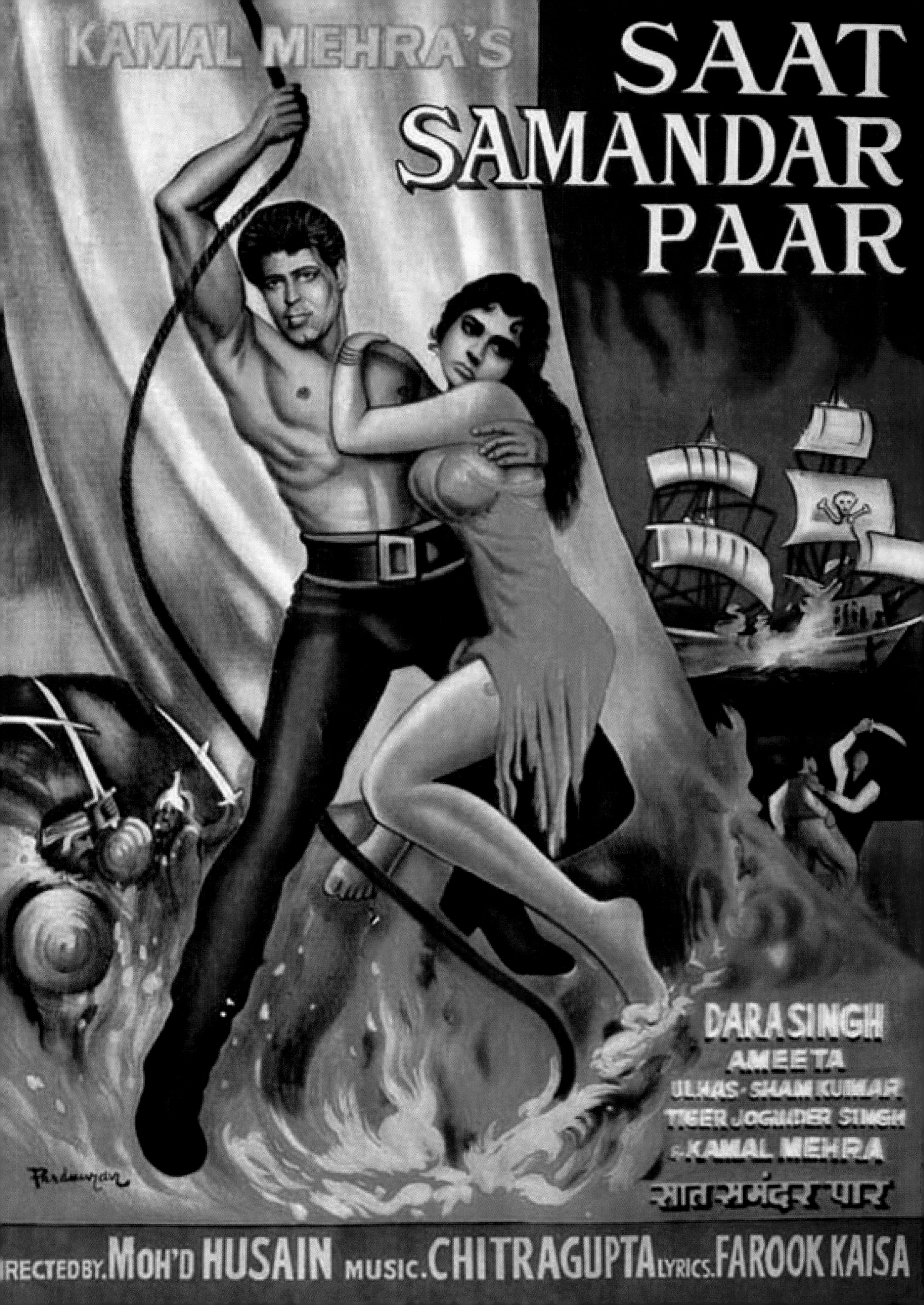
KAMAL MEHRA'S
SAAT SAMANDAR PAAR
DARA SINGH
AMEETA
ULHAS · SHAM KUMAR
TIGER JOGINDER SINGH
& KAMAL MEHRA
सात समंदर पार
IRECTED BY. MOH'D HUSAIN MUSIC. CHITRAGUPTA LYRICS. FAROOK KAISA

निर्माता निर्देशक **शशी कपूर**

in collaboration with Gorky Studios, Moscow
in EASTMANCOLOR by Prasad Film Laboratories, Madras

(फाईनेन्स)

आशीया फिल्म्स प्रा. लि.   संगीत लक्ष्मीकान्त-प्यारेलाल   गीत **आनन्द बक्शी**

Photo Offset Printed by : DNYANSAGAR LITHO PRESS, BOMBAY-4.

Bollywood Posters

नविन निश्चल · रेखा और डॅनी
मुकुल इन्टरप्राईजेस
राम दयाल का
ज़ोरो
दिग्दर्शक
शीबु मित्रा
संगीत
कल्याणजी
- आनंदजी
गीत
वर्मा मलीक
Seth STUDIO

A RAKESH ROSHAN FILM
KRRISH
MUSIC RAJESH ROSHAN
a sequel to
KOI MIL GAYA
FILMKRAFT PRODUCTIONS (INDIA) PVT. LTD. PRESENTATION
UNIQUELY Singapore

DRONA

A FILM BY GOLDIE BEHL

EROS INTERNATIONAL PRESENTS A ROSE MOVIES PRODUCTION "DRONA" A FILM BY GOLDIE BEHL
COSTUME DESIGN ANAITA SHROFF-ADJANIA WRITERS GOLDIE BEHL, JOYDEEP SARKAR EDITOR SHYAM SALGAONKAR LYRICS VAIBHAV MODI
MUSIC ASHU-DHRUV PRODUCTION DESIGNER TANIA BEHL DOP SAMEER ARYA PRODUCED BY SHRISHTI ARYA, SUNIL LULLA DIRECTED BY GOLDIE BEHL

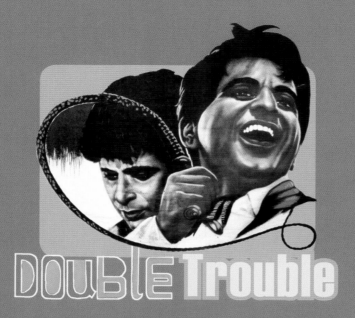

DOuBLE Trouble

In many ways, playing a double role is seen as one of the highpoints of a star's career. It means that the producer of the film is willing to bet on the audience wanting a double dose of the star since she or he – though more often he than she – will turn up in almost every shot.

And so it is the near-legendary superstar Amitabh Bachchan who has probably played the largest number of double roles in the film industry. At last count he has essayed double roles in 17 films. He is also one of the two superstars of Bollywood who played a triple role in *Mahaan* (1983, S Ramanathan). The other was Dilip Kumar who played three characters in *Bairaag* (1976, Asit Sen). Both films flopped.

On the eve of the release of *Lal Badshah* (1999, KC Bokadia), Amitabh Bachchan said he did not believe that playing a double role had anything to do with star value. "I've never thought about it in that way. As far as I'm concerned it seems like an interesting visual exercise. And it provides a challenge for the actor. Whether the audience sees it that way is a different matter."

To present a double role credibly, a star must split this persona down the middle, apportioning unique mannerisms to either side. Dev Anand, who brought two very different versions of himself to the screen in *Hum Dono* (1961, Amarjeet), points out that it is a challenge to play a double role, "because you are offered a double role only when you are a star. And you are a star in Indian cinema only when you are identifiable, you are associated with a certain style. You have to learn how to play around within the parameters of audience expectation."

Hindi films have usually crafted double roles so that the two on-screen identities are completely opposed to each other. One will be shy and retiring, the other bold and outgoing. In *Ram aur Shyam* (1967, Chanakya), Ram (Dilip Kumar), a young man brought up in the country, is portrayed as virile and outgoing. His twin brother Shyam (Dilip Kumar), brought up in a palace, has had his spirit broken by those who want to control his wealth. A similar fantasy of rich versus poor, country versus court, is played out in *Seeta aur Geeta* (1972, Ramesh Sippy), with the female star Hema Malini playing twin sisters. In the poster of the film, the difference is evident. One of the sisters swings from the fan; the other simpers coyly. Sridevi reprised much the same role in *Chaalbaaz* (1989, Pankaj Parashar).

All these films have one thing in common: the rescue of the rich sibling by the poor sibling. This reinforces the socialist view that the poor are sane and healthy while the rich are effete and decadent. It also offered some measure of consolation to those who were sitting in the stalls of the cinemas.

In the end, both sides of the star will be restored to wholeness; in other words, both will become the star. This may seem difficult. Will we now tell one from the other? In *Mahaan*, for instance, the senior Bachchan has his wife and children restored to him, the dour police officer begins to lighten up a little and the frivolous stage actor settles down to a life of responsibility. In other words, all three achieve the status of "Man". But the film ends at this point and we are released from our thrall to the myth of the doppelganger.

The poster makers had a special problem here: how to indicate these differences. If the director had been kind enough to supply some noticeable difference, such as a moustache or a different hairstyle, this might be used. When a star played father and son, silver streaks amid the black were often enough.

In rarer cases such as *Lamhe* (1991, Yash Chopra), in which Sridevi played mother and daughter, the generation gap was suggested by a change in clothing from traditional Indian to western. It was often enough to simply say it in words: "Vinod Khanna in a double role." So powerful has the phrase become that it works in Hindi and Urdu transliteration as well, now divorced from its linguistic roots.

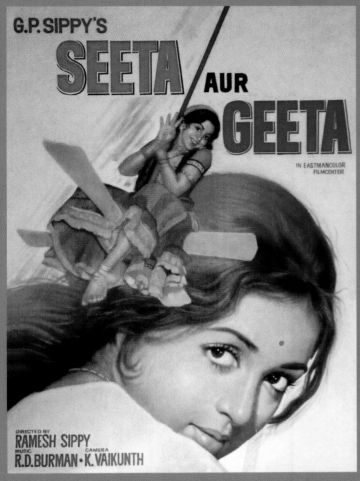

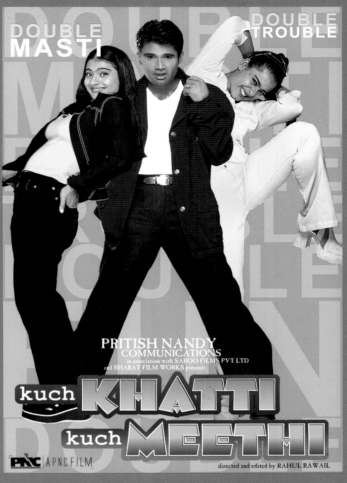

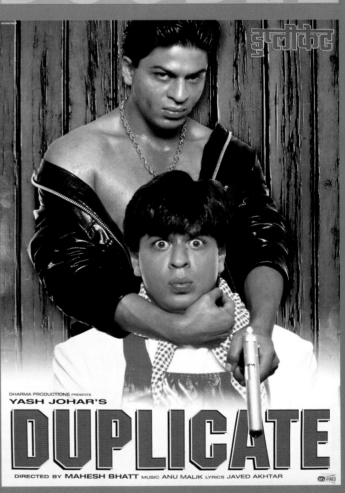

ART OF THE POSTER

For most of its life, the poster has not been recognized as art. It has generally been a participant in the commercial life of some other product and so it was not thought much of by those who believed in art for art's sake. It was always designed to be accessible in intent and meaning, thus deprived of the multiplicity of nuance seen as the hallmark of great art. It was mass-produced and so the notion of the visceral connection between the artist and his creation, the umbilical link between hand and medium was always missing. Even those artists who designed posters do not seem to have kept "originals".

Finally, the poster has never been placed in the sacred context of "art". If art galleries and museums are normally quiet spaces, with the objects in them offered for veneration, this is because the line can be drawn between temple and museum, between deity and artwork. When the dividing line is drawn between the mundane and the sacred, the poster was to be found in the realm of the mundane, competing with a cacophony of colour around it.

Thus it is probably no surprise that it took the arrival of post-modernism, with its emphasis on the quirky and its anti-sacramental approach to art, for the poster to acquire its own place in the pantheon of the collectible, which in turn has contributed significantly to its status as an independent art form. It is easy in hindsight to point to the works of Toulouse-Lautrec who created posters for nightclubs, or those of the legendary Indian painter MF Husain who created posters for films that people have now forgotten. What is often not remembered is that one could buy original posters from the heyday of Le Chat Noir for a few francs on the Rive Gauche and that there were few takers for these.

At a time when art was being judged by academic standards, Bollywood posters were being designed without subtlety. But then the designers who created them were aware that they had to compete with an environment that was already rich in colour.

That was not the only reason why these posters were – and often still are – so highly coloured. The Bollywood poster must also work against the flattening effects of a tropical sun. By mid-morning the light pours down. By midday they are powerful streams that drain colour from everything. By evening some subtlety may return to the hues around us but through the course of the day, when the engines of commerce drag millions of people past these posters, they must struggle with the sun. The colours bleach over time and so they must be laid on with a heavy hand.

Another reason for the use of melodramatic colours was that the films themselves eschewed subtlety for a mad melange of emotions. Here form followed content. Consider the basic plotline of *Amar Akbar Anthony* (1977, Manmohan Desai).

Kishen Lal (Pran) is a driver employed with Robert (Jeevan), a smuggler who asks him to take the drop for a crime. In return Robert promises to take care of his wife, Bharati (Nirupa Roy) and three sons. On his return Kishen Lal finds his wife suffering from the most popularly portrayed disease of commercial cinema, tuberculosis, and his sons starving. Kishen Lal takes his revenge; he robs his employer and takes his sons along with him. The wife gets left behind as she is at a doctor's clinic. Chased by his boss's goons, he leaves his sons at a park and tells them to wait for his return. However, his car meets with an accident and falls off a cliff. He survives, though the police mistakenly assume that he and his sons are dead.

Back at the park the sons get separated from each other. A Muslim tailor adopts the youngest and names him Akbar, a police inspector takes in the eldest child and retains his original name, Amar, while a Catholic priest takes in the middle child and renames him Anthony.

Bharati hears of the "death" of her husband and children, wanders out into a storm and loses her sight. The boys grow up. Amar (Vinod Khanna) becomes a police officer, Akbar (Rishi Kapoor) a *qawwal* or a singer of devotional Islamic/Sufi songs and Anthony (Amitabh Bachchan), a small-time crook. Kishen Lal also kidnaps Jenny (Parveen Babi), the daughter of Robert, as part of his revenge. And the titles haven't rolled yet.

If you offered this as a brief to the designer of a poster, what would he do? How would he indicate exactly what was going on in this film? How would he prepare an audience? What elements of this story would go into the poster?

In the prelapsarian days when filmmaking was still a seat-of-the-pants affair, when marketing was not considered the most important factor determining the fate of the film, it was the art department of studios that designed the posters. This was staffed by unlettered and often untrained workers, under the eye of a supervisor who might be trained in commercial art.

Then again, he might not. He might belong to a family of poster designers, serve an apprenticeship under a master designer, learn some of his skills and then move on to another studio. In the days before high-resolution photography, digital prints and outdoor printing on Flex, the process began with a series of stills from the film (in the better organized studios) or random headshots of the cast. These would be marked over with a grid. Like a contour map, the grid would thicken in density where more detail was required and thin out across those places where broad swathes of colour would suffice. The better poster painters would need fewer lines and use their imaginations.

This grid would then be transferred to a huge stretch of canvas and painted in. For the smaller posters, those on lamp-posts, for instance, the rectangle was re-oriented. The hoarding used the landscape format (where the width was greater than the height), whereas the poster used the portrait grid (where the height was greater than the width). Design was mainly about arranging faces in the most appealing manner possible.

Anyone could be entrusted with the job of designing a poster of a film, as the near-legendary director Kidar Sharma found, when he was an indigent husband and father in Mumbai. In order to make both ends meet, he had accepted "an offer to paint posters for the publicity officer of the New Theatres in order to make some money".

There was one small room [in his apartment] which I used as my studio for painting and writing. I could not afford to buy an easel or palette so I had to make do without these essentials. I used the floor for mixing paint, and I would also spread the poster on the floor to work on it, since I could not afford a drawing board. One day when I had finished a 40" x 60" poster, I let it dry on the floor. It was a large face of Umashashi the big star. The next day, when I went to this small room, I was shocked to find her face looking like Charlie Chaplin's. There was an addition of a Hitler-type mustache on her upper lip. Soon the mystery was solved by a child's giggle. Vikram [his young son] had spilled some black colour on the floor, smeared his tiny feet with wet paint and just walked across the face of the big star.

From THE ONE AND LONELY KIDAR SHARMA by Kidar Sharma

One of India's foremost artists, Maqbool Fida Husain also told his biographer, Ila Pal, of the problems of making posters in the early days of the studios. It was a time when there was not much work for artists and paintings did not sell regularly. The middle-class did not have the disposable incomes of today nor the inclination to buy art. When Husain heard that the actor-director Nazeer was making a film called *Society*, the artist went to him and asked for work.

"Five days for eleven panels and I had to do them single-handed. I could work only during daylight hours for his studio did not have any electric light in the compound. To enlarge the photographs in the conventional way with the help of graphs would guarantee my failure so without any delay, I spread them on the ground and started working free-hand.

"It is amazing how much we can train our sensory organs, how well they adapt to our needs. Expert surveyors can spot a gap of even a few inches from a great distance... a painter can do a lot more with two eyes and two hands. In the process of making hoardings, I trained my eyes, rather one eye, to see constantly the rest of the painting in the distance and my hand simultaneously to make the necessary adjustments in scale. This helped me overcome the problems of foreshortening and of relating what is in the distance to the area one was working on. I do not recollect many occasions when I have changed, repainted, or corrected my original drawing."

From BEYOND THE CANVAS: AN UNFINISHED PORTRAIT OF MF HUSAIN by Ila Pal

Pal also records the time Husain had to complete a 40-foot cut-out of film star Durga Khote who was appearing in a Marathi film. An impoverished artist, he had no access to a space large enough for this, except for the street. He could only use its expanse for four hours, between midnight when the trams stopped running and 4am when the first one would roll down the tracks again. He spread his canvas across the road and set to work. At five minutes to four, the cut-out was ready. This was the slapdash way in which a film's primary attempt at building an audience was created. The cut-out, now lost to posterity, may well have been brilliant as it was created by a master draftsman of the calibre of Husain. Other posters would have been worked on by other artists, nowhere as skilful or talented.

Leave your primary advertisement in the hands of an unproven amateur or even an artist who might give priority to the aesthetic over the commercial? Today, in an age which has placed a high premium on the concept of marketing, the thought seems almost suicidal. After all, the poster was the first shot at getting the public's attention.

In the beginning, this public was largely elite since cinema began, again, not as an art form but as a novelty. Just as Victorian audiences gathered in fashionable drawing rooms for displays of the marvels of electricity, early audiences all over the world grouped together just to convince themselves that the system worked. But soon the idea of telling a story caught on and the stories began to be advertised. These threw up their own modes of narrative and styles of acting – early cinematic acting now looks like a series of unlikely grimaces reproduced at the wrong speed – and those who could make the most of the new medium became stars. Eventually, it was the actors and not the content of the films that drew in audiences from every strata of society. Film viewing became the competition to theatre and it was obvious that the elite would want to patronize, or be seen as patrons of, the elder art form.

Film scholar Ashish Rajadhyaksha draws a direct line between the work of the painter Raja Ravi Varma (1848–1906) and the films Dadasaheb Phalke made. If Varma had given faces to the pantheon of Indian gods, goddesses, sages and spirits, Phalke was responsible for bringing these to celluloid. The lithograph images would have infiltrated his imagination since they were already quite common in Hindu homes, especially in the *puja ghar*, the part of the house that was set aside for worship of the gods. The problem, of course, is that this artistic predecessor of a film industry we have learnt to be proud of, was a very bad painter. He was sentimental in his choice of themes, patriarchal in the depiction of men and women, unimaginative in his choices and repetitive in his constructions.

But he was well loved in his time. "While he is completely susceptible to attacks of aesthetic incompetence," writes Ashish Rajadhyaksha, "yet his impact on what we can today call industrial art remains massive. From calendars to posters, to the design and packaging of small-scale indigenous consumer products, to street-corner art including cheap film posters, we see this impact."

बी. आर. चोपड़ा
कृत

कर्म

संगीत
आर. डी. बर्मन
पटकथा · संवाद
पं. मुखराम शर्मा

JAGDISH PHOTO · PROCESS

KARM

The ordinary man in the street bought his chromolithographs since they reflected almost exactly his own way of thinking. Ravi Varma is admired too because his works have now acquired the status of "national treasures". (This description applies to any work of art that is over a hundred years old. The tag often works against its commercial value since, by government rules, it cannot be exported.) Varma's women are of particular significance. They faithfully recreated models of beauty described in Sanskrit poetry. They were fair-skinned, fish-eyed, big-breasted and had wide hips so that they might "walk like the elephant". Many filmmakers drew inspiration from early imaginative encounters with these well-endowed and unimaginative women.

Right from childhood I have been an admirer of the paintings of the great Indian artist Raja Ravi Verma. In his paintings he depicts a young and ethereally beautiful Ganga, scantily clad, as divine as spiritual perfection. So also the paintings of another famous Indian artist, Kanu Desai, whose work in those days was available in prints. I was an avid collector of Kanuji's prints and in them too I saw a similar Ganga, young and scantily clad, and as spotlessly pure and beautiful as the Ganga at its source. These visions of Ganga by great Indian painters stayed alive and breathing in my mind and formed the yardstick in my search for a girl to play Ganga. Fortunately, painters like Raja Ravi Verma and Kanu Desai painted scantily clad, nubile beauties as their vision of Ganga at a time when there weren't any holier-than-thou film journalists around to vilify them and sling mud at them. Like the rat pack did when Raj Kapoor tried to present a similar vision onscreen!

Raj Kapoor to Bunny Reuben in FOLLYWOOD FLASHBACK: A COLLECTION OF MOVIE MEMORIES

In tandem with the development of a market for film posters, much has been written on them too. However, while the poster is mined for its sociological meaning, very little attention has been paid to its aesthetic value. This is because, like other products of human endeavour, most posters are not very good. The collage was often created without much thought given to balance, proportion or harmony. Sometimes it seemed as if scraps of older posters had been torn out and stuck together to create a new one. The human figures seemed to lack perspective or were distorted to appear more attractive. This happened frequently with the creation of anatomically impossible women whose breasts were "augmented". The grid would often produce images acceptable only when seen in the context of the photographs that were used. Familiar faces would thus turn into facsimiles of themselves. However, in a nation that is obsessed with cinema, this did not really matter. As long as there was some reasonable resemblance, the poster could go up and the punters would turn up at the turnstiles, eager for their share of the stardust generated within.

Then again, often, there was no relationship between the quality of the poster and the quality of the film it represented. *Mughal-e-Azam* may have been one of the greatest Bollywood movies ever made but its posters were not very inspiring. *Kahin Aar Kahin Paar* (1971, Maruti) is a film in whose strength the producers had so little faith that they tried to dress up the posters to resemble the successful film *Aar Paar* (1954, Guru Dutt). The modifier "*Kahin*" in all the samples shown here is deliberately not as eye-catching as the other words. However, it is still a powerful poster. Obviously, in this case, the designer outstripped the rest of the team in terms of aesthetic ability.

And then there was plagiarism, a failing that Bollywood has been unable to distance itself from, even as it protests that the name Bollywood is derivative. The source material was often the Hollywood poster, a trend that continues with little sign of abating. When the story and sometimes entire shots in the film are lifted, the poster naturally follows. Even where there is no direct link between the films, an element may be "borrowed". The latest example of this, at the time of writing, is the use of the tagline "Sometimes the greatest journey is the distance between two people", from *The Painted Veil* (2006, John Curran) for *U, Me aur Hum* (2008, Ajay Devgan). The impact of James Bond film posters can be seen clearly in the poster for *Kahin Din Kahin Raat* (1968, Darshan), on page 200.

THEIRS NOT TO REASON WHY: The art of the handmade poster is all but finished. Now computers will do what the poster painters did. A lone painter soldiers on

BISWAJIT · SAPNA
BISWAJIT · HELEN
PRAN · NADIRA · MALIKA
JOHNNY WALKER
कहीं दिन कहीं रात
کہیں دن کہیں رات
SHREE KRISHNA FILMS
कहीं दिन कहीं रात

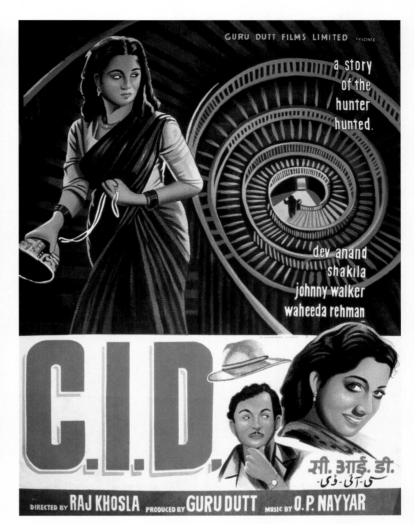

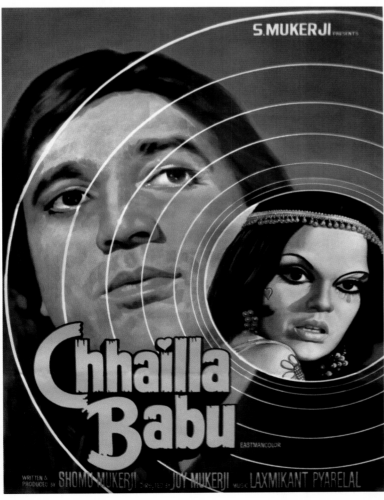

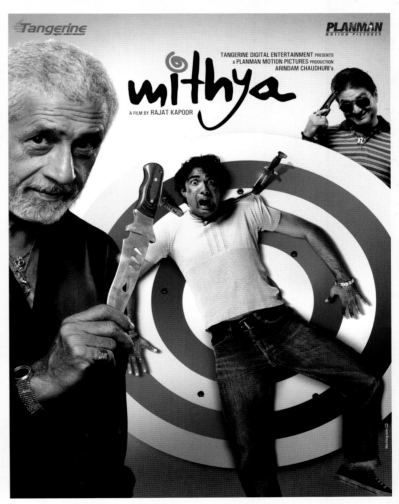

NO SMOKING

EROS INTERNATIONAL PRESENTS "NO SMOKING" AN BIG SCREEN ENTERTAINMENT PVT. LTD. AND VISHAL BHARDWAJ FILMS PRODUCTION

STARRING JOHN ABRAHAM AYESHA TAKIA PARESH RAWAL RANVIR SHOREY MUSIC BY VISHAL BHARDWAJ LYRICS GULZAR EDITOR AARTI BAJAJ ART DIRECTOR WASIQ KHAN DIRECTOR OF PHOTOGRAPHY RAJEEV RAVI

EXECUTIVE PRODUCER SANJEEV JOSHI LINE PRODUCER INDERJIT CHADHA CO PRODUCER SUNIL LULLA PRODUCED BY KUMAR MANGAT VISHAL BHARDWAJ WRITTEN & DIRECTED BY ANURAG KASHYAP

WWW.NOSMOKING-THEFILM.COM

STATUTORY WARNING CIGARETTE SMOKING IS INJURIOUS TO YOUR · EARS · FINGERS · FAMILY · MIND · SOUL

JAVED AKHTAR & CHANDAN SIDHWANI PRESENT

DIL CHAHTA HAI

AN EXCEL ENTERTAINMENT PRODUCTION

दिल चाहता है

www.dilchahtahai.com

MUSIC	LYRICS	CO-PRODUCER	PRODUCED BY	STORY, SCREENPLAY, DIALOGUE & DIRECTION
SHANKAR EHSAAN LOY	JAVED AKHTAR	PRAVIN TALREJA	RITESH SIDHWANI	FARHAN AKHTAR

It would be harsh to blame the artists alone for this. They worked in improbable conditions, as the excerpts from Kidar Sharma's autobiography and MF Husain's biography show. There would be star egos to contend with (a universal problem it might seem; Hollywood star Bette Davis once told the skin magazine *Playboy*: "I will never be below the title").

Even when the poster uses the combined skills of two artists such as Anjolie Ela Menon and Manjula Padmanabhan, there could be problems. "Anjolie Ela Menon and I were very close those days – we both lived in Bombay and I used to spend a lot of time at her house," says Padmanabhan. "She's the kind of artist who knows her own strengths well – so when Muzaffar Ali asked her to design the poster she knew she'd need help with the boring design bits – you know, the title-typography, the paste-up and stuff. That's all I did: I just helped her execute her concept for the poster.

"Her initial idea was an actual painting of Rekha as *Umrao Jaan*, in profile. She did one in the style of a Mughal miniature but life-size – it was really beautiful. But Muzaffar thought the man-in-the-street wouldn't recognize the star. So we played it safe. Anjolie cut out a photograph of Rekha in that famous pose – seated on the floor with her ivory-gold skirt spread out around her – and positioned the figure against a background she painted in her signature colour of that time, a melancholy dusk-brown."

Today, all aesthetic analysis of the poster relies on nostalgia, itself an important part of the whole enterprise of kitsch. Posters that look "hand-painted" have greater cachet than those that used photographs. This would have surprised the poster painters whose holy grail was a photographic realism. Almost in a perfect reversal of this process, the poster for the nostalgia-laden superhit film *Om Shanti Om* (2007, Farah Khan) used a computer programme to recreate the hand-painted look. The death of the poster painters' skill seems to concern the middle class deeply but not enough to recognize that these men worked for a pittance, without union protection or standardized wages, and that their art remains largely anonymous even today.

Yet, there is evidence that the poster has found its niche in the art market. Neville Tuli, founder, chairman and CEO of Osian's Connoisseurs of Art, described the power of a poster to journalist Amrita Shah: "Its [the poster's] energy, its raw ability to communicate and excite, its mix of reality and imagination, its ability to transform noble ideas into crass images and yet maintain an innocence, its ability to transverse all sorts of contradictions and still remain uniquely coherent."

Bollywood posters have begun to attract the kind of attention that other popular culture and industrial art forms deserve. Although there has been almost no serious attempt at establishing an aesthetic or even a realistic commercial value scale for them, they are now everywhere: in drawing rooms, in art galleries and even in museums. The poster and hoarding seem to be dying. While India is beginning to become design-conscious and India Inc now acknowledges the power of marketing, the poster has a slow fade-out. Hoardings are now used to advertise new television shows, not only films.

But while poster designers have become a lot more sophisticated, often with degrees in design and hot shops starring Mac computers and huge amounts of software, they are still treated as supernumeraries, often the last to be paid. This may be because the very dynamics of selling a film have been reinvented dramatically as the target audience itself has changed. Now, every film has several media partners attached and together the newspaper, the television channel, the news site and the dedicated website attempt to create a buzz around the film. Posters are no longer the herald of a new film. But this is likely to make posters even more collectible and even more valuable. As the poster begins its slow fade-out, the hand-painted posters of the past with their idiosyncratic colouring and beautiful hand-lettering will become increasingly precious.

Mirchi Movies Limited presents
a Miracle Cinefilms and Serendipity Films production

WHO YOU let in
can CHANGE
your life

NASEERUDDIN SHAH   DIMPLE KAPADIA   SAIF ALI KHAN   BOMAN IRANI

BEing CYRUS

a film by homi adajania

EXECUTIVE PRODUCER: A P PARIGI | PRODUCERS: AMBIKA A HINDUJA, DINESH VIJAN, RAMAN MACKER, MUNNISH PURII | MUSIC: SALIM SULAIMAN

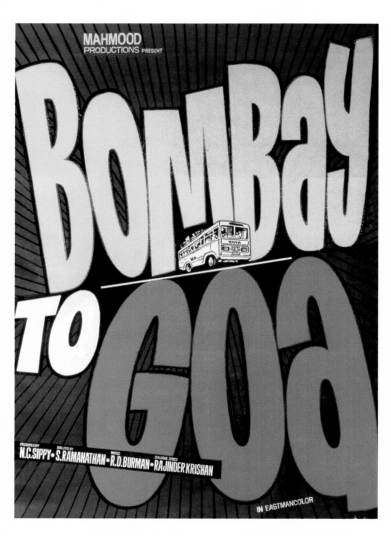

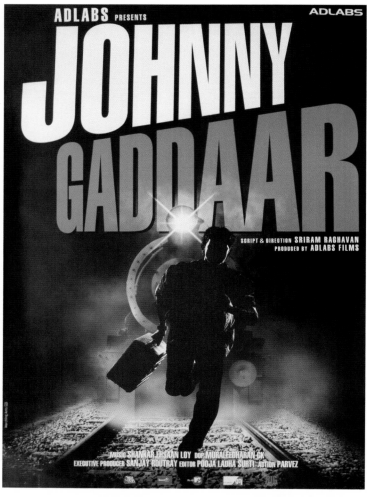

RAJINDER KUMAR PRESENTS
NANDA
RAJESH KHANNA
IN
ROSE MOVIES'
THE
EASTMANCOLOR
VASUDEO
PHOTOGRAPHED & DIRECTED BY
RAVEE NAGAICH
MUSIC
RAHUL DEV BURMAN
LYRICS
ANAND BAKSHI
PRODUCED BY
RAMESH BEHL
ट्रेन
APSARA ARTS

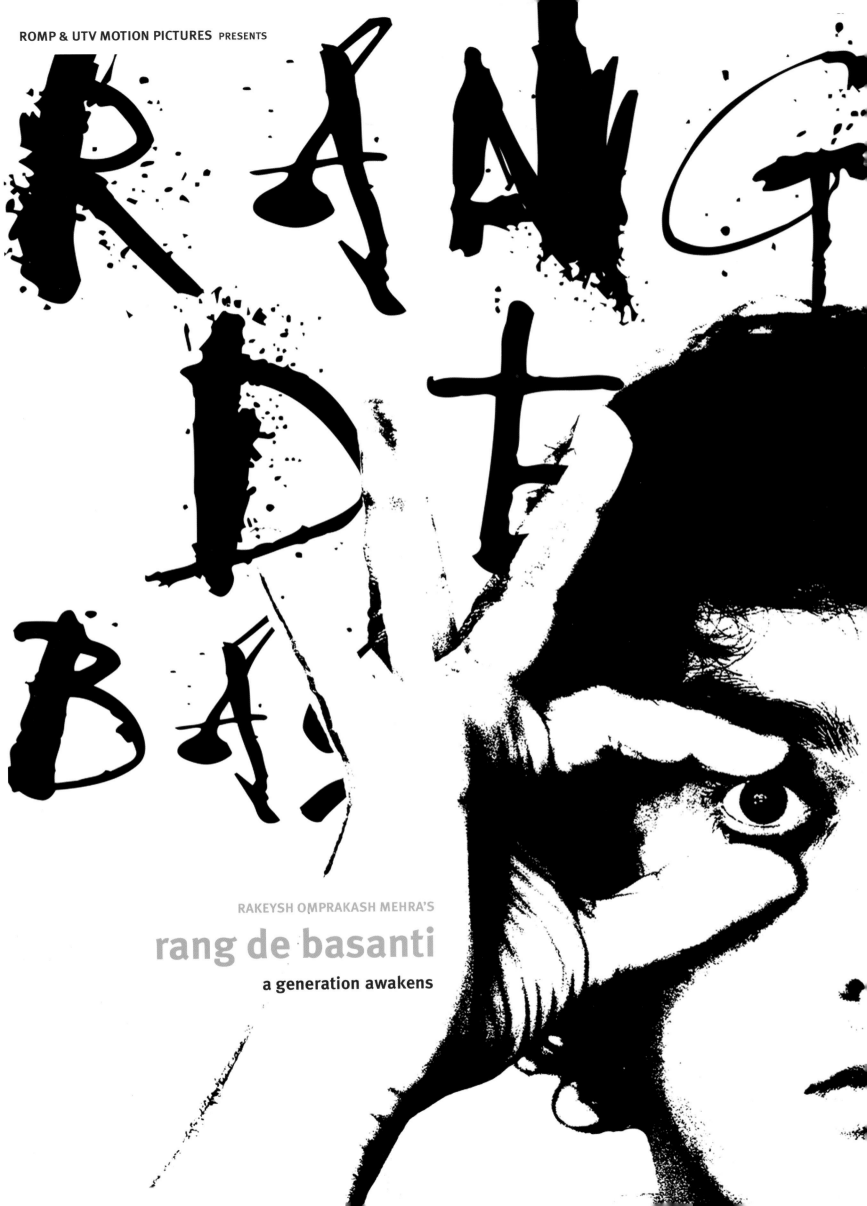

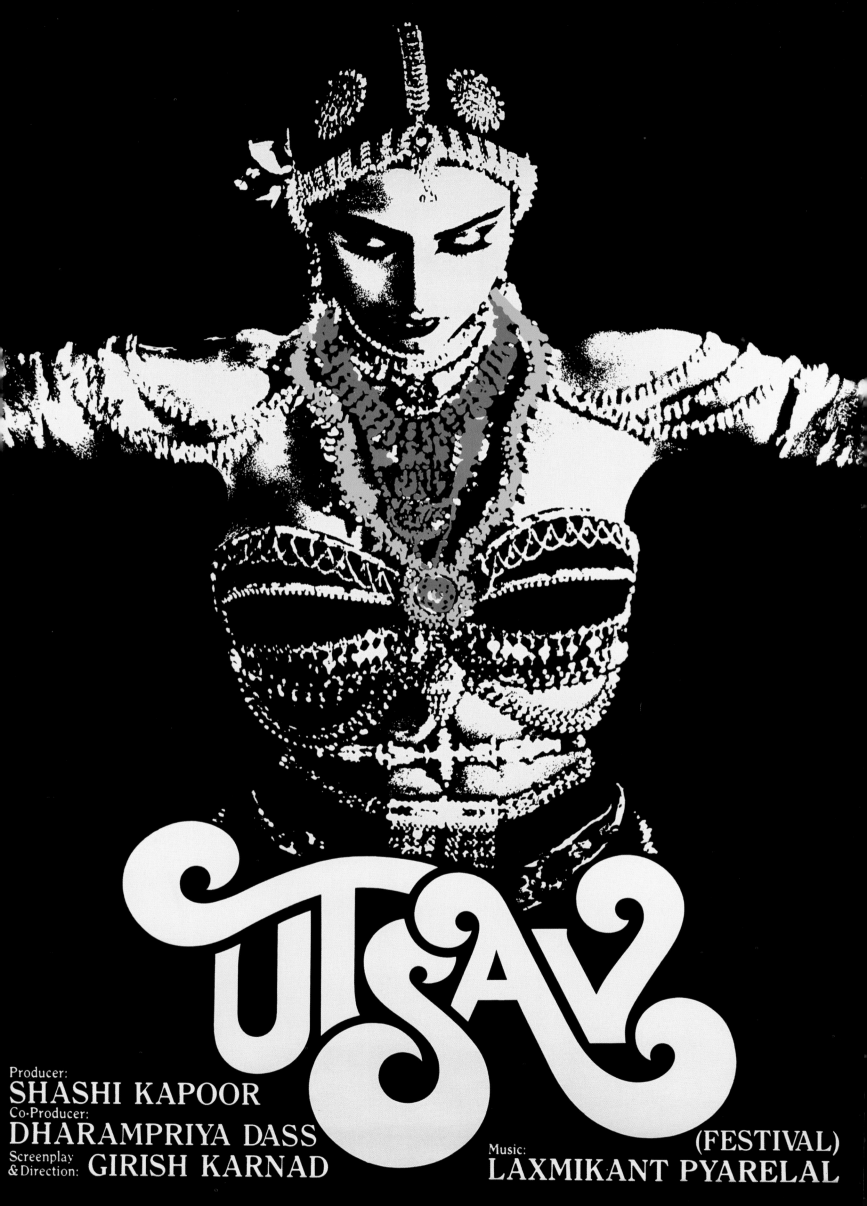

SHASHI KAPOOR presents **UTSAV** (FESTIVAL)

Co-Producer: Screenplay and Direction: Music:

DHARAMPRIYA DASS GIRISH KARNAD LAXMIKANT PYARELAL

PROCESSED & PRINTED BY : NENSEY OFFSET TEL. : 872 6127 / 872 8H3

INDEX

Italics indicate illustrations

BIBLIOGRAPHY

Anand, Dev, *Romancing With Life,* 2007

Burra, Rani, *Ashok Kumar: Green to Evergreen,* 1990

Das Gupta, Chidananda, *The Painted Face: Studies in India's Popular Cinema,* 1991

Dwyer, Rachel, *Filming the Gods: Religion and Indian Cinema,* 2006

Haham, Connie, *Enchantment of the Mind: Manmohan Desai's Films,* 2006

Kabir, Nasreen Munni, *Bollywood: The Indian Cinema Story,* 2001

Kesavan, Mukul, *The Ugliness of the Indian Male,* 2008

Pal, Ila, *Beyond the Canvas: An Unfinished Portrait of MF Husain,* 1994

Pinney, Christopher, *Photos of the Gods: The Printed Image and Political Struggle in India,* 2004

Reuben, Bunny, *Follywood Flashback: A Collection of Movie Memories,*1993

Sarkar, Kobita, *You Can't Please Everyone! Film Censorship: The Inside Story,*1982

Sharma, Kidar, *The One and Lonely Kidar Sharma,* 2002

POSTERS WITH TITLES IN HINDI

Anand 18, Ajnabee 76, Ajooba 181, Aradhana 155, Asoka 115, Bees Saal Baad 201, Garam Khoon 189, Jai Hanuman 135, Kahin Din Kahin Raat 200, Neel Kamal 178, Nigahen 137, Parivar 151, Tere Mere Sapne 151, Zorro 183

PHOTO CREDITS

Special thanks to Wahid, Sajid and Zahid Mansoori (Mini Market, Mumbai) for helping to kick-start this project. To the National Film Archive of India, Pune, for their collection. To Dhun Cordo and Rahul Nanda for sharing their timeless designs. And to Shobha & Chaitanya Sant and Sucharita Sengupta for providing an all-access pass to their creativity. Every reasonable attempt has been made to identify and contact owners of copyright. The authors would like to extend their gratitude to the following rights holders for supporting this project:

2008 Warner Brothers Pictures India Pvt Ltd, *Chandni Chowk to China*

Aamir Khan Productions Pvt Ltd (Aamir Khan), *Lagaan*

AAN Productions (Jaffer Hussain), *Raat Aur Din*

Adlabs Films Ltd (Sunir Kheterpal), *Bluffmaster, Johnny Gaddaar*

AJ Dos Ani & A Rahim, *Kaala Jaadu*

Ajantaa Arts, *Yaadein*

Amar Chhaya (Surinder Kapoor), *Shehzada*

Ambika Chitra (Rajiv RL Suri), *Parwana*

Aparajita Sinha, Joy Bimal Roy, Yashodhara Roy, *Do Bigha Zamin, Parakh, Sujata*

Ashutosh Gowariker Productions Pvt Ltd, *Jodhaa Akbar, Swades*

Bimal Roy Memorial & Film Society (Rinki Bhattacharya), *Do Bigha Zamin, Parakh, Sujata*

BR Films (BR Chopra, Ravi Chopra), *Karm, Pati Patni Aur Woh, Waqt*

Cineye Films (Basu Chatterji), *Us Paar*

Dharma Productions (Karan Johar), *Duplicate, Kal Ho Naa Ho*

Eros International Presents Big Screen Entertainment (Kumar Mangat and Vishal Bhardwaj), *No Smoking*

Excel Entertainment Pvt Ltd, *Dil Chahta Hai, Don*

Filmalaya Pvt Ltd (Rono Mukerji), *Haiwan*

Filmistan Studio (Jasraj Purohit), *Anarkali, Ek Armaan Mera, Munimji, Nagin*

Filmkraft Productions (India) Pvt Ltd (Rakesh Roshan), *Krrish*

Film-Valas (Shashi Kapoor), *Ajooba, Utsav*

FK International (Feroz Khan), *Dharmatma*

Geetanjali Pictures (Bela Mukherjee), *Bees Saal Baad, Khamoshi*

Gold Entertainment Pvt Ltd (Manilal V Shah), *Kab? Kyoon? Aur Kahan?*

Gouri Films Pvt Ltd (Ramanand Sagar), *Prem Bandhan*

Grand Master (Vikas Sahni), *Nigahen*

Guru Dutt Films Pvt Ltd (Arun Dutt), *Aar Paar, Chaudhvin Ka Chand, CID, Kagaz Ke Phool, Mr & Mrs 55, Pyaasa, Sahib Bibi Aur Ghulam*

JP Films (JP Dutta), *Umrao Jaan*

Kapur Films (Manmohan Kapur), *Apna Khoon*

Kardar Productions, *Shahjehan*

Madan Movies (Mahindra R Bohra), *Jai Hanuman*

Mahal Pictures Pvt Ltd (Tajdar Amrohi), *Pakeezah, Razia Sultan*

Mehboob Productions Pvt Ltd (Iqbal Mehboob Khan), *Andaz, Anmol Ghadi, Mother India*

Minerva Movietone (Mehelli Modi), *Jhansi Ki Rani, Pukar, Sikandar*

Mirchi Movies Ltd (Munish Purii), *Being Cyrus*

Movie Tee Vee Enterprises (Kewal Suri), *Dilruba, Kahin Aar Kahin Paar, Kavi Kalidas, Laila Majnu, Naag Panchami, Parivar, Saat Samandar Paar, Shaheed, Zehreela Insaan*

Mukta Arts Ltd (Subhash Ghai), *Iqbal*

Mukul Entertainers (Nirmal Kanta Sabharwal), *Zorro*

Narsimaha Enterprises (Boney Kapoor), *Company*

Nasir Husain Films Pvt Ltd (Mansoor Khan, Nuzhat Khan), *Teesri Manzil, Zamaane Ko Dikhana Hai*

Navketan Enterprise (Sushma Anand), *Tere Mere Sapne*

Navketan International Films (Dev Anand), *Guide, Jewel Thief, Tere Ghar Ke Samne*

New World Pictures (BR Pachisia), *Jaal*

Nishi Productions (Raj Kumar Kohli), *Nagin*

NN Sippy Productions (Pravesh Sippy), *Shatranj*

NP International (NP Singh), *Warrant*

Planman Motion Pictures (Arindam Chaudhuri and Shubho Shekhar Bhattacharjee), *Mithya*

Pramod Films (Prateek Chakravorty), *Naya Zamana*

Pritish Nandy Communications Ltd, *Chameli, Kuch Khatti Kuch Meethi, Sahib Biwi Ghulam*

Raj Khosla Films (Anita Puri), *Do Chor*

Raj Lakshmi Productions, *Veer Abhimanyu*

Raj Rishi Films (Rishi Raj), *Aayega Aane Wala, Balram Shri Krishna, Delhi Junction, Do Shatru, Pocket Maar, Rocket Tarzan, Veer Bhimsen, Yaadon Ki Zanjeer*

Rajshri Productions Pvt Ltd (KK Barjatya), *Bombay to Goa, Dil Tera Deewana, Toofan*

Ram Gopal Chitra Mandir (Ram Gopal Gupta), *Mahapavan Teerth Yatra*

Ramsay Productions (India) (Tulsi Ramsay), *Ek Nanhi Munni Ladki Thi*

Red Chillies Entertainment (Sanjiv Chawla), *Asoka, Om Shanti Om*

RK Films & Studios (Randhir Kapoor), *Awara, Barsaat, Bobby, Jis Desh Men Ganga Behti Hai, Mera Naam Joker, Satyam Shivam Sundaram, Shree 420*

Rose Movies (Madhu Behl), *The Train*

Rose Movies (Shrishti Arya), *Drona*

RS Arts, *Naag Shakti*

RS Entertainment (Ramesh Sippy), *Bluffmaster*

RSE Orion Films, *Chandni Chowk to China*

Rupam Pictures Pvt Ltd (Romu Sippy), *Anand*

Sagar Art International (Ramanand Sagar), *Ankhen*

Sahyadri Films (Shyam Benegal), *Bhumika, Junoon, Manthan*

Salma Nariman Irani, *Don*

Seven Arts Pictures (Madan Mohla), *Raja Jani*

Shakti Films (Ashim Samanta), *Ajnabee, An Evening in Paris, Aradhana, Howrah Bridge*

Shankar Movies (Raj Kumar Kohli), *Bees Saal Baad*

Shemaroo Entertainment Pvt Ltd, (Raman Maroo), *Benaam, Chhailla Babu, Ek Baar Mooskura Do, Faulad, Kaajal, Manorama Six Feet Under, Mere Huzoor, Neel Kamal, Sachaa Jhutha, Shakka, The Great Gambler*

Shilpakar (Harish Shah), *Mere Jeevan Saathi*

Shree Krishna International (Suneel Darshan), *Kahin Din Kahin Raat*

Shreya Creations Pvt Ltd (Sheel Kumar), *Struggler*

Shringar Films Ltd (Shyam Shroff), *Chakravyuha, Chalti Ka Nam Gadi, Sindbad, Alibaba and Aladin, Swami*

Sippy Films Pvt Ltd (Sascha Sippy, Shaan Uttamsingh), *12 O'Clock, Raaz, Seeta Aur Geeta*

SLB Films (Sanjay Leela Bhansali), *Saawariya*

SPE Pvt Ltd (Uday Singh), *Saawariya*

Sterling Investment Corporation Pvt Ltd, *Mughal-E-Azam*

Sun Rich Productions, *Ek Kadam*

Suresh Productions (Suresh Ramanaidu), *Dildaar*

Tips Industries Ltd (Ramesh Taurani), *The Legend of Bhagat Singh*

Trade Guide Media (Baran Adarsh, Taran Adarsh), *Putli Bai*

Trimurti Films Pvt Ltd (Rajiv Rai Sachdev), *Deewar, Johny Mera Naam*

Uday Enterprises (Bela Segal, Deepak Segal), *Sajan*

Uttam Chitra (Romu Sippy), *Koshish*

UTV Motion Pictures, *Jodhaa Akbar, Khosla Ka Ghosla, Rang De Basanti*

Wadia Films Pvt Ltd, *Mela*

Yash Raj Films Pvt Ltd (Yash Chopra), *Chandni, Dhoom 2, Sawaal*

Zar Productions (Ravindra Zar), *24 Ghante*

Zar's International (Ravindra Zar), *Garam Khoon*

Zee Entertainment Ltd (Mohammed Zaki), *Raksha*